Real Food, Real Simple

Real Food, Real Simple

80 DELICIOUS PALEO-FRIENDLY, GLUTEN-FREE
RECIPES IN 5 STEPS OR LESS

TAYLOR RIGGS, R.D.N.

Founder of Simply Taylor

PAGE STREET
PUBLISHING CO.

PAGE STREET
PUBLISHING CO.

Copyright © 2017 Taylor Riggs

First published in 2017 by
Page Street Publishing Co.
27 Congress Street, Suite 105
Salem, MA 01970
www.pagestreetpublishing.com

Distributed by Macmillan, sales in Canada by The Canadian Manda Group.

20   19   18   17   1   2   3   4   5

ISBN-13: 978-1-62414-337-3
ISBN-10: 1-62414-337-7

Library of Congress Control Number: 2016940924

Cover and book design by Page Street Publishing Co.
Photography by Allison Lehman

Printed and bound in China

Page Street is proud to be a member of 1% for the Planet. Members donate one percent of their sales to one or more of the over 1,500 environmental and sustainability charities across the globe who participate in this program.

Contents

INTRODUCTION

Growing up, I was fortunate enough to have a family who sat down at the table for dinner together almost every night. Despite our busy schedules, my mom and dad (who both worked full-time) and my older sister Lindsay and I, would almost always sit down for dinner together at the end of the day. Friends would often join us when they were at our house after school or basketball practice, and Lindsay and I always laugh remembering one of her friends asking, "So wait, you guys do this *every* night?" Yep. We did. And we never really knew anything different.

But our meals were never complicated or ornate. Now, don't get me wrong; my mom has always been a great cook, as was her mom (my "Nanny") and some of her brothers and sisters, too. So I grew up with some pretty great influences in the kitchen. But my mom was also aware that getting a 5-star meal on the table every night for a busy family just wasn't going to happen (ummm hi, can anyone relate?), so we had staples. Taco night, spaghetti night, salad night, etc., and of course, the still-standing Friday family pizza night. They were simple, easy and (mostly) healthy meals that made it into the weekly rotation and didn't take hours or endless complicated steps to prepare. Plus, there was still always a little room left for indulgence. I don't think I totally realized it until later in life, but this is how I learned that eating healthy didn't have to mean spending hours on end in the kitchen every night. Hence where "Real Food, Real Simple" truly began.

When I was ten years old, I got extremely sick one weekend. My dad took me to the doctor, and what we thought was just the flu turned into a whirlwind of a week spent at Children's Hospital. When I finally went home, I had a new diagnosis of type 1 diabetes, an autoimmune disease that affects the endocrine system. Whaaaaat does that even mean? Well, essentially it meant that my body had attacked itself, and that my pancreas no longer produced insulin, a vital hormone needed to regulate blood sugar. Type 1 diabetes (which is much different from type 2) didn't run in our family and none of us knew anything about the disease until that week, but it drastically changed all of our lives as we knew them, and especially mine. Insulin injections, finger pricks, carbohydrate counting, highs, lows and everything in between. Nutrition became a huge part of my life, not as a choice, but as a necessity.

From then on, I had to be extremely careful about what I ate, when I ate it and how much medicine it would take for my body to tolerate it. I ate a generally healthy diet as an adolescent and teenager and always had a pretty good hold on controlling my diabetes, but it wasn't until I started studying nutrition in college that I really began to pay closer attention to how certain foods made me feel and how they truly affected my blood sugar levels.

Sometime between my second and third year of school at The Ohio State University, I started hearing more and more about the Paleo diet and the effects it could have on blood sugar and diabetes. I did my research and decided to jump in, full-force, following every rule there was about a strict, Paleo diet. And the results were incredible. My blood sugars were more stable than they had ever been, I was taking less insulin than I ever had in the past and I felt pretty darn amazing physically. I followed this way of eating pretty intensely for the next year or so and things were going so well that I decided to start a full-on Paleo recipe blog, which some of you may remember as *Taylor Made it Paleo*. I had so much fun experimenting with new recipes and different ways I could put a healthier spin on some of my old favorites.

Somewhere along the way, I started experimenting with other foods that weren't necessarily considered "okay" on a strictly Paleo diet (a little cheese, some occasional gluten-free treats), and I would often post these across my social media channels and on the blog. At first, it was tough. I was doing so well health-wise on a strict Paleo diet and was almost afraid of going off of that plan, thinking that things might somehow take a drastic turn for the worse. But, the more I started slowly re-introducing things and taking note of how I felt when I ate them and how my blood sugar reacted, the more I found myself appreciating the balance and the freedom that came without the "Paleo" label. I eventually made the decision to change the name of my blog (now *Simply Taylor*), and to sort of start fresh again. For the most part, people were really supportive and appreciated the fact that I was exploring different foods and finding out what worked best for *me* personally. In fact, many followers reached out to tell me that they had had a similar experience.

Most of the recipes on my blog now can still be categorized as Paleo (as are the recipes in this book), and I still preach many of the keys to a Paleo diet to my readers, followers and nutrition clients. I just don't go out of my way to scream the Paleo "label" from the mountaintops anymore. I think the key principle to take away from a Paleo diet is that it's all about choosing real, whole foods and giving your body the nutrients it needs. I think it's more important to focus on adding the good stuff than restricting or eliminating the "bad," and working to find a balance that fits your life.

My goal is to share recipes made from whole, nutrient-dense foods, and inspire people to eat healthier by making that as simple as possible to do. As a Registered Dietitian Nutritionist, I would never want anyone to think that I would force a certain diet upon them, or that there is a one-size-fits-all approach to nutrition. *There isn't.* I want people to, like I did, find what works best for them and their own bodies and discover a place of balance when it comes to food. Whether that be Paleo, vegan, gluten-free, full-gluten or anywhere in between, I'm all for it. *Find what works for you and roll with it.*

Many of the recipes in this book are, or can easily be, transformed into something that works for everyone, not just those following a Paleo diet. For example, if you don't eat meat, substitute beans or cashews for chicken in the Easy Chicken Vegetable Stir-Fry (page 46). If you tolerate cheese, sprinkle it on top of the Italian Spaghetti Squash Boats (page 62). These recipes are meant to be *guides,* not bibles, and I encourage you to use them as such. To me, cooking is all about turning on some music, getting creative and putting your own spin on things. Maybe the recipe calls for 1 teaspoon of hot sauce, and that just doesn't cut it for you. Add more! Season things to your liking. Replace red peppers with yellow if that's more your style. Use chocolate chips instead of blueberries. Whatever it might be, go for it!

So I hope you'll enjoy these recipes, have fun experimenting with them and try something new along the way. Eating well doesn't have to be difficult, and I hope this book will help to prove that.

Taylor Riggs

Making Healthy Eating Easy

This book is all about making healthy eating easy and enjoyable, so I have a few tips to help you do just that before you dive in:

1. Keep it real

Choose real, whole foods as often as you can. What do I mean by this? Fresh fruits, vegetables, lean proteins, nuts, seeds and unprocessed foods that are as close to their natural form as possible. Our bodies are meant to consume foods made from the earth, not from factories; foods rich in nutrients, not in chemicals; and foods that make us feel good, not bad. So whenever possible, start by picking real, fresh foods and go from there. Your body will thank you!

2. Help you help yourself

I always find it helpful to spend at least one hour on meal preparation each week. No, this doesn't mean you have to prepare all of your meals for the week in full on Saturday or Sunday or portion out all of your lunches into individual plastic containers. It just means taking a little bit of time each weekend to make your life *way* easier during the week by doing a little bit of prep work for yourself. By doing something as simple as chopping a few peppers or onions to have on hand for dinners during the week or cooking a big batch of cauliflower rice to have as a base for your lunches, you will save yourself a ton of time (and stress) when it comes to weekday meals. I promise! Whether you're getting home late from work or the kids have a soccer game, having less work to do for a meal makes it 100% more likely to actually happen. Make a goal to set aside just *one hour* for this each week and I promise you'll notice a big difference!

3. Be prepared

The above being said, how will you know what you need to prep for the week if you don't know what you want to make? You won't! So try making a list at the beginning of the week of what meals you'd like to have and the ingredients you'll need to make them. This way, when you go grocery shopping, you won't be aimlessly walking around the store putting things into your cart that you don't need; or worse, forgetting items you do need, leading to an extra grocery trip during the week. (The horror!)

Making a grocery list immediately sets you up for a great week because it gives you a built-in action plan. Try writing your dinner ideas for the week down on a calendar and hang it on your refrigerator, or make notes of your weekly meals on your phone. I even think it's fun to create a photo album on my iPhone titled, "This Week's Meals" and save pictures/recipes for each day so I can have a visual and something easily accessible if I need to look up ingredients while I'm at the store. Being prepared means setting yourself up for success!

4. Embrace the power of leftovers

I believe there are two types of people in this world: those who love leftovers and those who don't (ha!). And I hope to one day show the latter that they are *really* missing out. Seriously! In fact, I think food often tastes even better the next day, since the flavors have had a little time to sink in and marinate. Plus, you can repurpose things in new ways. Have chicken lettuce wraps for dinner on Monday? Throw the extra filling into an egg scramble for breakfast on Tuesday. Voila! Two healthy meals for the price (and work) of one *and* you didn't waste any food. It's a win-win!

5. Create your own healthy environment

Have you ever heard someone say that if you keep healthy food around, you'll eat healthy food? And if you keep junk food around, that's what you'll eat? Well it's true!

One of the most valuable concepts I learned during my dietetic internship at Ohio State is that our environment plays a *major* role in the health decisions we make. For example, if we open our refrigerator and see sodas and candy bars front and center, with water and fruit shoved into the bottom back corner, the first option for many of us is going to be the candy bar. Why? Because it's readily available, easily accessible and, well, it looks and tastes good. Plus, the fruit has to be washed, peeled and prepared, so from a convenience standpoint, the candy bar wins.

But, what if we made a few small changes to our environment? For example, what if we pre-washed the fruit, put it into an open bowl and moved it to the front of the refrigerator at eye level and put the candy and soda in the corner down below? Or better yet, what if we eliminated the candy and soda all together? Leaving the fruit as the only option?

We can't always control every piece of our environment. But, there are simple efforts we can make to help put ourselves in better situations when it comes to making healthy decisions in our everyday lives. Tired of being tempted by doughnuts at work meetings? Try eating breakfast before you get to the office. Want to stop hitting up the vending machine for your 3 p.m. snack? Leave your cash at home and keep a bag of almonds in your purse. Small changes can have big outcomes and can help make the healthy choices easier.

6. Find Your Balance

I have discovered from personal experience how important finding balance is to a healthy lifestyle. It can be easy to have an "all-or-nothing" personality when it comes to diet or exercise or work or school, but I've found that it's actually okay to not be *all* in. It's okay not to eat a 100% Paleo diet. It's okay not to do killer workouts seven days a week. The important thing that I continue to reiterate is that you find a balance that works for *you*. Whether that means you follow the "80/20" rule, you eat Paleo, you eat vegan, you eat whatever the hell you want; by all means do it. If it's a *lifestyle* that's healthy and treats your mind and body well, I'm a fan of it.

one

MORNINGS
OVER EASY

They say breakfast is the most important meal of the day, and I am certainly not one to argue that!
Starting the day off on a healthy note 100% sets the tone for the rest of the day for me. If I eat well in
the morning, it automatically makes me want to eat well at the rest of my meals. Plus, who doesn't *love*
breakfast food? Even if you aren't a "morning person," the recipes in this chapter will make you want
to jump out of bed and get the day started–promise! If you like your morning meal savory, the
Sundried Tomato and Artichoke Quiche (page 15) is for you. If you prefer a sweeter start, don't miss the
California Acai Bowl (page 23) or the Pumpkin Spice Waffles (page 28).

SUNDRIED TOMATO *and* ARTICHOKE QUICHE

Anytime my family gets together for breakfast or brunch, I always bring a quiche. It's simple and delicious, and no one can resist the soft and flakey almond flour crust. The sundried tomatoes and artichoke hearts make this version burst with flavor, and the creamy goat cheese has everyone coming back for seconds!

YIELD: 6–8 SERVINGS

1/1/23 oK

INGREDIENTS

For the Crust

2 cups (224 g) almond meal

¼ tsp sea salt

1 large egg

2 tbsp (28 g) coconut oil, melted
(plus more to grease the dish)

For the Filling

1 cup (180 g) artichoke hearts   *frozen, drained*   *chopped spinach*

½ cup (80 g) sundried tomatoes

1 tsp garlic, minced

4 large eggs

1 cup (240 ml) unsweetened almond milk

2 tbsp (2 g) fresh basil, roughly chopped

2 oz (57 g) goat cheese, optional

DIRECTIONS

Preheat the oven to 375°F (190°C).

1. Combine all of the crust ingredients in a food processor and pulse on high for 30 seconds, or until the dough starts to ball up and pull away from the sides of the bowl.

2. Press the dough evenly into the bottom and up the sides of a 9-inch (23-cm) pie or quiche dish lightly coated with coconut oil. Add the artichoke hearts, sundried tomatoes and garlic evenly into the dish.

3. In the food processor, blend the eggs and almond milk for 10–15 seconds to combine, then pour the mixture over the tomatoes and artichokes. Sprinkle the basil and goat cheese (optional) over the top.

4. Bake for 45–50 minutes, or until the egg is set in the middle.

> **Tip** I used sundried tomatoes bottled in olive oil and canned artichoke hearts for convenience in this recipe, but feel free to use fresh if you'd like!

Saturday Morning
PANCAKES

Because what could possibly kick off the weekend better than a big stack of pancakes? The sweetness from the banana and coconut flour makes this version perfectly yummy as is, but the simplicity of the recipe also makes it super versatile for whatever goodies you decide to mix in on your own. The possibilities are endless!

YIELD: 4 PANCAKES

1.08 cal each
good - texture not as fluffy as reg. pancake but still tastes good 1-28-23

INGREDIENTS

2 large eggs

½ medium banana, mashed

3 tbsp (45 ml) unsweetened almond milk

1 tbsp (21 g) honey

1 tsp vanilla extract

¼ cup (28 g) coconut flour

½ tsp baking soda

Coconut oil to grease the skillet

Toppings (optional)

Fruit

Nut butter

Maple syrup

DIRECTIONS

1. Whisk together the eggs, banana, almond milk, honey and vanilla in a large bowl.

2. Add the coconut flour and baking soda and continue whisking to form a batter.

3. Taking about ¼ cup (85 g) at a time, drop the batter onto a large skillet lightly coated with coconut oil over medium-low heat to form the pancakes.

4. Cook on one side for 2–3 minutes (or until the pancake is firm enough to flip), then flip using a spatula and cook completely on the opposite side, about 2 more minutes.

5. Top with fruit, nut butter and maple syrup as desired.

> **Tip** To mix things up, add blueberries, chocolate chips or cinnamon to the batter for a punch of extra flavor.

Sweet Potato, Bacon *and* Brussels Sprout Hash

Who says you can't have Brussels sprouts for breakfast? This savory hash makes it easy to get a serving or two of veggies in before you even start your day and is filling enough to keep you satisfied all morning. Plus, the vibrant colors of this dish just scream "fresh!"

Yield: 4–5 servings

. . . .

Ingredients

3 strips of bacon *finely diced ham*

1 tsp garlic, minced

1 cup (100 g) yellow onion, diced

1 lb (450 g) Brussels sprouts

2 medium sweet potatoes, diced into 1 inch (2.54 cm) cubes

~~4~~ 5–6 large eggs

Salt and pepper, to taste

Directions

Preheat the oven to 350°F (176°C).

1. Cook the bacon in a large skillet over medium heat until crispy, about 2–3 minutes per side. Remove the bacon from the skillet and set aside.

2. In the same skillet, add the garlic, onion, Brussels sprouts and sweet potatoes and sauté for 10–12 minutes, or until the Brussels sprouts and sweet potatoes become tender.

3. Crack the eggs over the top of the hash and sprinkle with salt and pepper.

4. Place the skillet in the oven and bake for 8–10 minutes, or until the eggs are cooked to your liking.

5. Remove the skillet from the oven and crumble the bacon over the top.

251 cal

Coconut Crêpes *Two Ways*

If you ask me, crêpes are the perfect vessel for just about anything. Sweet, savory and everything in between, crêpes pair well with almost any filling, like the Spicy Chorizo and Almond Butter Banana versions shown here. Try a batch of each when entertaining so guests can have their pick of sweet or spicy!

YIELD: 4 CRÊPES

INGREDIENTS

For the Crêpes

1 whole egg

3 egg whites

3 tbsp (21 g) coconut flour

1 tbsp (14 g) coconut oil, melted (plus more for coating the pan)

2 tbsp (30 ml) unsweetened almond milk

For the Spicy Chorizo Filling

½ lb (225 g) hot chorizo sausage

½ cup (50 g) yellow onion, finely chopped

½ cup (63 g) red pepper, finely chopped

Fresh cilantro, to garnish

For the Almond Butter Banana Filling

1 tbsp (14 g) coconut oil

3 bananas, sliced into small pieces

1 tbsp (21 g) honey

2 tbsp (32 g) almond butter

2 tbsp dark chocolate chips, optional

DIRECTIONS

1. Combine all of the crêpe ingredients in a food processor and blend for 15–20 seconds.

2. In a medium skillet lightly coated with coconut oil, pour ¼ of the crêpe mixture into the middle of the pan and swirl the pan around gently to form a thin, even layer of batter. Cook the first side for about 30 seconds, then carefully flip and remove after 15 seconds on the second side. Repeat with the remaining batter.

3. For the Spicy Chorizo filling, brown the chorizo in a skillet over medium heat, about 2–3 minutes. Then add the onion and pepper and continue to sauté until the chorizo is completely cooked, about 3–4 minutes. Fill each crêpe with the chorizo mixture and garnish with cilantro.

4. For the Almond Butter Banana filling, heat the coconut oil over medium heat and add the banana slices and honey. Sauté for 2–3 minutes. Fill each crêpe with a layer of the banana mixture, then drizzle with almond butter. Sprinkle in the chocolate chips (optional).

Tip Since the crêpes are so thin, they are also easy to burn if you don't pay close attention. Be sure to keep one eye on the crêpe and one eye on the clock to ensure even cooking.

California Acai Bowl

This creamy, refreshing bowl is my go-to in the summertime, and it's *bursting* at the seams with nutrients and antioxidants from all of the fresh fruit ingredients. Just one look at its vivid colors will have you California dreaming all day long about its sweet, fruity flavors!

YIELD: 1 bowl

INGREDIENTS

2 (3.5-oz [110-g]) frozen acai packets, unsweetened

1 cup (140 g) frozen blueberries

1 banana

¼ cup (60 ml) unsweetened almond milk

Toppings (optional)

Strawberries

Blueberries

Kiwi

Hemp, chia or flax seeds

Nut butter

Cacao nibs

DIRECTIONS

1. Run the acai packets under hot water for 10–15 seconds to soften.

2. Add all the ingredients to a high-speed blender and blend until smooth, about 30 seconds.

3. Pour into a bowl and add toppings as desired.

Tip Though the base of the bowl is made up of mostly fruit, you can easily add nut butter or hemp seeds to up the protein and healthy fat content and make it a meal!

Honey Almond Flax Loaf

This loaf is *so* nutrient-dense, and with all its sweet spices it is one of my favorite recipes, especially during the fall. With a base made from almonds and flax seed, you'll have no problem getting a big dose of healthy fats with just one slice. I love enjoying a sliver with a little nut butter or ghee and a warm cup of coffee while sitting on the back porch in the crisp autumn air!

YIELD: 10–12 SLICES

INGREDIENTS

2 cups (224 g) almond meal

½ cup (60 g) ground flax meal

1 tbsp (8 g) ground cinnamon

1 tsp turmeric

1 tsp sea salt

½ tsp ground ginger

Dash of black pepper

1 tsp baking soda

4 large eggs

¼ cup (84 g) honey

2 tbsp (28 g) coconut oil, melted

2 tbsp (30 ml) full-fat, canned coconut milk

1 tsp vanilla extract

DIRECTIONS

Preheat the oven to 350°F (176°C).

1. Combine the almond meal, flax meal, spices and baking soda in a small bowl.

2. In a large mixing bowl, combine the eggs, honey, coconut oil, coconut milk and vanilla.

3. Slowly add the dry ingredients to the wet, mixing until a batter forms. Pour the batter evenly into a 4 ½ x 8 ½ inch (11 ½ x 21 ½ cm) (or similar) loaf pan lined with parchment paper.

4. Bake for 30–35 minutes, or until a toothpick comes out clean in the center.

Tip If you don't have parchment paper, just lightly coat the inside of the bread pan with a little coconut oil to prevent sticking.

Rutabaga HASH BROWNS

This recipe gives good old-fashioned hash browns a modern-day (healthy!) makeover and they make the perfect addition to any breakfast spread. Pair them with bacon and eggs over easy for the picture-perfect farmer's breakfast.

YIELD: 4–5 SERVINGS

yum! so tasty + fast

INGREDIENTS

1 rutabaga, skin removed

1 tbsp (15 ml) olive oil

1 tsp garlic, minced

½ tsp sea salt

Pepper to taste

Eggs (optional)

DIRECTIONS

1. Using a vegetable peeler, make short, quick motions to peel off small pieces of the rutabaga. Repeat for the entire vegetable.

2. Heat the olive oil in a large skillet over medium heat and add in the garlic.

3. Add the rutabaga, salt and pepper and sauté for 5–7 minutes. At this step you may also crack eggs over the rutabaga and cover to cook to your desired yolk consistency.

102 cal. w/out eggs

Tip If you don't have a vegetable peeler, you can also use the wide holes of a cheese grater to make hash browns with a finer texture.

Pumpkin Spice WAFFLES

Though pumpkin season is technically in the fall, I guarantee that you (and everyone you know) will want to eat these waffles year-round! The warm spices and pumpkin pair so perfectly with a drizzle of maple syrup, and the almond butter adds an extra richness to the sweet and spicy autumn flavors.

YIELD: 6–8 WAFFLES

INGREDIENTS

1 cup (240 g) pumpkin puree

1 cup (256 g) almond butter

2 large eggs

2 tbsp (30 ml) maple syrup

1 tsp vanilla extract

1 tbsp (7 g) ground cinnamon

1 tbsp (8 g) arrowroot flour, *cornstarch or wheat flour*

1 tsp ground ginger

¼ tsp ground cloves

¼ tsp sea salt

1 tsp baking soda

Coconut oil for greasing waffle iron

Toppings (optional)

Banana slices

Maple syrup

Ghee

DIRECTIONS

1. Combine all of the ingredients (except the coconut oil) in a large bowl and mix well to form a batter.

2. Drop ⅓ cup (113 g) of batter onto a waffle iron lightly coated with coconut oil, and cook according to the iron instructions.

3. Repeat with the remaining batter.

4. Add desired toppings.

321 Cal / waffle!

Tip These waffles are freezer-friendly, so they're great for making at the beginning of the week and then popping into the toaster in the morning for a quick breakfast!

Kitchen Sink
VEGGIE FRITTATA

This colorful, savory dish is not only a crowd-pleaser for breakfast, but it can be a fantastic dinner meal as well. Plus, it takes just minutes to prepare and is a great way to clean out the fridge with whatever veggies you have on hand from the week's grocery or farmers' market haul!

YIELD: 4–6 SERVINGS   *4—16-23 Good*

INGREDIENTS

6 large eggs

⅓ cup (80 ml) unsweetened almond milk

Salt and pepper to taste

½ cup (48 g) mushrooms, finely chopped

½ cup (63 g) red pepper, diced

½ cup (63 g) green pepper, diced

Coconut oil to grease the dish

Arugula for topping, optional

+ .25 cup feta

DIRECTIONS

Preheat the oven to 325°F (162°C).

1. In a medium bowl, whisk together the eggs, almond milk, salt and pepper.

2. Add the mushrooms and peppers to the bottom of a 9-inch (23-cm) pie dish lightly coated with coconut oil.

3. Pour the egg mixture over the veggies to fill the pie dish.

4. Place the dish into the oven and bake for 40–45 minutes or until the egg mixture is fully cooked.

5. Remove from the oven and top with arugula (optional).

> **Tip** Place the pie dish on a baking sheet before cooking for easier handling.

Cranberry Orange Scones

Sometimes you need a little treat to go with your morning tea or coffee! The zest from the orange gives these scones a little something special and will fill your whole house with a sweet, citrus aroma all day long!

YIELD: 8 SCONES

INGREDIENTS

2 cups (224 g) almond meal

1 tsp baking soda

¼ tsp sea salt

1 large egg

2 tbsp (28 g) coconut oil, melted

1 tbsp (21 g) honey

1 tbsp (15 ml) fresh orange juice

1 tsp orange zest

¼ cup (30 g) dried cranberries

DIRECTIONS

Preheat the oven to 350°F (176°C).

1. Combine the almond meal, baking soda and salt in a small bowl.

2. In a large bowl, combine the egg, coconut oil, honey, orange juice and orange zest. Add the dry ingredients to the wet and mix to form a dough. Fold in the cranberries.

3. Form the dough into a ball, then flatten it into a disk about 6 inches (15 cm) in diameter and ½ inch (1.27 cm) thick.

4. Cut the disk into 8 triangular pieces (like a pie) and place them on a baking sheet lined with parchment paper. Bake for 10 minutes.

Cinnamon Raisin Bread

1-14-23 dr -

This Cinnamon Raisin Bread has been the most popular recipe on my blog for years, and for good reason. The almond flour gives it just the right amount of density, while keeping it light and fluffy at the same time, and you'll get a pop of sweetness in every bite with the raisins. I'll bet you can't eat just one slice!

YIELD: 10–12 SLICES

. . . .

INGREDIENTS

2 cups (224 g) almond meal

2 tbsp (16 g) ground cinnamon

1 tsp baking soda

¼ tsp sea salt

5 large eggs

¼ cup (84 g) honey

¼ cup (56 g) coconut oil, melted

2 tsp (20 ml) vanilla extract

¼ cup (40g) raisins

DIRECTIONS

Preheat the oven to 350°F (176°C).

1. Combine the almond meal, cinnamon, baking soda and salt in a medium bowl.

2. Combine the eggs, honey, coconut oil and vanilla in a large bowl.

3. Slowly add the dry ingredients to the wet, and continue mixing. Stir in the raisins.

4. Pour the batter into a 4½ x 8½ inch (11½ x 21½ cm) (or similar) loaf pan lined with parchment paper and bake for 25–30 minutes, or until a toothpick comes out clean in the center.

much longer - if jiggles its not baked even if tester comes out clean

> **Tip** Not into raisins? This bread tastes great on its own!

SHAKSHUKA

If you're looking for the ultimate savory-style breakfast, Shakshuka is your answer. But the tomato base paired with eggs makes it perfectly suitable for a meal at any time of the day. And not to mention, it's gorgeous! The bold color of the tomato and pop of green from the fresh cilantro make this both a feast for the stomach and the eyes! So if you need a tasty brunch recipe that looks (and tastes) like a million bucks, but don't have a lot of time to spare, look no further!

YIELD: 4 SERVINGS

INGREDIENTS

2 tbsp (30 ml) olive oil

1 tsp garlic, minced

1 cup (100 g) yellow onion, finely chopped

½ cup (63 g) red pepper, finely chopped

1 (28-oz [794-g]) can whole, peeled tomatoes

1 tsp cumin

1 tsp paprika

1 tsp sea salt

½ tsp black pepper

¼ tsp cayenne pepper

4 large eggs

Cilantro to garnish

DIRECTIONS

Preheat the oven to 350°F (176°C).

1. Heat the olive oil in a large skillet over medium heat and add the garlic, onion and red pepper. Sauté until the veggies are tender, about 3–5 minutes.

2. Add the tomatoes and spices and cook for another 8–10 minutes.

3. Crack the eggs on top of the tomato and veggie mixture and place the skillet in the oven to bake for 8–10 minutes, or until the eggs are cooked to your liking.

4. Garnish with cilantro.

two

EFFORTLESS ENTRÉES

Healthy meals don't have to be difficult, and they definitely don't have to be tasteless either. The main dishes in this chapter pack plenty of flavor and, of course, take just five steps or less to prepare. Whether you're looking for simple staples like Nanny's Spaghetti Sauce and Meatballs (page 54) or something a little more exotic like Asian Chicken Lettuce Wraps (page 65), there's a little something for everyone when it comes to these effortless entrées.

Sweet Potato Noodles with Kale, Onion and "Cheese" Sauce

yum! 3/19/23

The sweet potato, kale and onion combo is one of my favorites in general, but the addition of the Cheesy Cashew Cream takes this dish to a whole new level of yum! Plus, it adds a little protein and plenty of healthy fats to the carbohydrates in the base, which is a winning combo for keeping you satisfied.

YIELD: 4–6 SERVINGS

INGREDIENTS

3 large sweet potatoes

1 tbsp (15 ml) olive oil

½ cup (50 g) yellow onion, finely chopped

6 cups (120 g) kale, roughly chopped

1½ cups Cheesy Cashew Cream (page 165)

DIRECTIONS

1. Spiralize the sweet potatoes into thin, spaghetti-like noodles.

2. Heat the olive oil in a large skillet over medium heat and add in the onion and kale.

3. Sauté until the onions start to soften and the kale begins to wilt, about 2–3 minutes.

4. Add the sweet potato noodles and continue to sauté until noodles are al dente, about 7–8 minutes, or until cooked to your liking.

5. Remove the pan from the heat and add the Cheesy Cashew Cream. Stir to combine.

Tip Not a kale fan? Try spinach or arugula in its place!

Spaghetti Squash
VEGETABLE PIZZA BAKE

This meal has been a favorite in our family for a few years now, and every time we make it for guests they immediately fall in love with it, too! The spaghetti squash serves as a unique crust alternative, and the pizza sauce combined with Homemade Basil Pesto and fresh veggies make this meal the ultimate comfort food.

YIELD: 4–6 SERVINGS

INGREDIENTS

1 large spaghetti squash

1 tbsp (15 ml) olive oil

2 large eggs

¼ cup (28 g) coconut flour

½ tsp sea salt

¼ tsp black pepper

1 (15-oz [425-g]) can pizza sauce

½ cup (120 g) Homemade Basil Pesto (page 166)

1 cup (125 g) red pepper, thinly sliced

1 cup (125 g) green pepper, thinly sliced

1 cup (100 g) red onion, thinly sliced

½ cup (40 g) mushrooms, sliced

1 tsp garlic, minced

Dried oregano and basil to taste

4 oz (113 g) fresh mozzarella cheese, thinly sliced, optional

DIRECTIONS

Preheat the oven to 400°F (204°C).

1. Cut the spaghetti squash in half lengthwise and remove the seeds. Drizzle the insides with olive oil and place face down on a baking sheet. Bake for 35–40 minutes, or until a knife slides easily into the back of the squash.

2. Remove the squash from the oven and allow it to cool completely. Once cool, remove the strings from the squash using a fork, holding the squash vertically and repeating a downward scraping motion starting from the top and moving toward the bottom.

3. Remove the excess water from the strings by pressing them against a fine strainer or in a thin layer between two paper towels.

4. In a large bowl, combine the squash, eggs, coconut flour, salt and pepper to form the crust mixture. On a baking sheet lined with parchment paper, form the mixture into a large crust, about ⅛ inch (0.3 cm) thick.

5. Bake for 20–25 minutes. Remove from the oven and spread the pizza sauce evenly over the crust, followed by the basil pesto, vegetables, garlic, seasonings and cheese (optional). Return to the oven for 10–15 minutes, or until the vegetables are slightly tender and the cheese has melted.

Tip The "crust" here isn't meant for you to pick up off of the plate. As the title describes, this dish is a bake, so don't be afraid to dig in with a fork!

MEXICAN *Fiesta* SKILLET

Taco Night was always (and still is) one of my favorites, but what isn't my favorite is all of the dirty dishes that tend to come along with it. That's why I created this one-pan Fiesta Skillet, which has totally been rocking my world lately. In fact, combining all of the components into one skillet enhances all of the spicy, zesty flavors!

YIELD: 4 SERVINGS

2-2-23   needed
Cauld but   seasonings as
I made it

INGREDIENTS

1 lb (454 g) boneless, skinless chicken strips

¼ cup (60 ml) olive oil

1 heaping tbsp (8 g) My Go-To Taco Seasoning (page 169)   I used ortega

1 cup (125 g) red bell pepper, thinly sliced

1 cup (125 g) green bell pepper, thinly sliced

½ cup (50 g) yellow onion, thinly sliced

1 cup (180 g) tomato, diced

½ cup (6 g) cilantro

Coconut Cauliflower Rice (page 87), to serve, optional

DIRECTIONS

1. Combine the chicken, olive oil and seasoning mix in a large bowl or gallon (3.8 L) plastic bag and mix to combine. Allow the chicken to marinate for several hours in the refrigerator. If you're short on time, you can skip the marinating step, but the flavors come in much stronger if you do it!

2. In a large skillet over medium heat, cook the chicken for 2–3 minutes on each side, or until it is almost cooked through completely.

3. Add in the peppers, onion and tomato and sauté with the chicken for 2–3 minutes.

4. Add the cilantro and continue to sauté, about 2 minutes.

5. Serve over Coconut Cauliflower Rice (optional).

Tip: Only have ground chicken on hand? Forego Step 1 and add the spices right to the meat in the skillet with 1 tablespoon (15 ml) of olive oil.

336 cal

Easy Chicken Vegetable Stir-Fry

My mom made stir-fry frequently when I was a kid, and I was never its biggest fan. Now I kick myself for wasting so many years disliking it! This one is now on an almost weekly rotation for me and I can't get enough of the sweet, tangy flavor and fresh, colorful ingredients. Pairing this dish with Coconut Cauliflower Rice (page 87) is a MUST!

YIELD: 4 SERVINGS

INGREDIENTS

1 lb (464 g) boneless chicken breasts, cut into 1 inch (2.5 cm) pieces

2 tbsp (30 ml) coconut aminos, divided

4 tsp (11 g) arrowroot powder, divided

1 tsp sea salt, divided

1 tsp honey

½ cup (120 ml) chicken broth

1 tbsp (15 ml) olive oil

1 tsp garlic, minced

1 tsp fresh ginger, grated

For Stir-Fry

2 cups (160 g) broccoli florets

2 cups (175 g) baby portabello mushrooms, sliced

1 cup (135 g) carrots, diced

1 cup (100 g) green bell pepper, thinly sliced

1 cup (100 g) red bell pepper, thinly sliced

1 cup (140 g) water chestnuts, roughly chopped

¼ cup (16 g) green onion, chopped

Coconut Cauliflower Rice (page 87), to serve

DIRECTIONS

1. Combine the chicken with 1 tablespoon (15 ml) coconut aminos, 2 teaspoons (6 g) arrowroot powder, ½ teaspoon sea salt and the honey in a medium bowl.

2. In another bowl, combine 1 tablespoon (15 ml) coconut aminos, 2 teaspoons (6 g) arrowroot powder, ½ teaspoon sea salt and the chicken broth.

3. Heat the olive oil in a large skillet over medium heat and add the garlic and ginger. Add the chicken and stir-fry until it is almost fully cooked through, about 3–4 minutes. Transfer the chicken to a plate.

4. In the same skillet, add the broccoli and sauté for about 3 minutes. Then add the rest of the vegetables, chicken and broth mixture and continue to sauté for 5–7 minutes, or until all the vegetables are tender.

5. Serve over Coconut Cauliflower Rice.

Tip Feel free to use any vegetables you have on hand in this dish, or make swaps as you please. Anything goes here! Try snap peas, yellow pepper, zucchini, etc.

Coconut Cashew Curry Soup

This warming curry soup is perfect for curling up with on a chilly winter evening, and it is a great meatless meal to incorporate into your routine. The raw cashews provide such substance and bulk to the already nutrient-rich soup, and the blended sweet potatoes and turmeric give it a bright, vibrant color that's sure to warm you right up!

YIELD: 6–8 SERVINGS

INGREDIENTS

1 tbsp (15 ml) olive oil

1 tsp garlic, minced

1 cup (100 g) yellow onion, finely chopped

1 tbsp (15 g) red curry paste

2 tbsp (16 g) turmeric

1 tsp sea salt

1 tsp coconut sugar (optional)

2 small sweet potatoes, cubed

2 (14-oz [385-ml]) cans full-fat coconut milk

3 cups (720 ml) vegetable broth

3 cups (60 g) kale, roughly chopped

1 cup (125 g) green pepper, finely chopped

1 cup (125 g) red pepper, finely chopped

1 cup (112 g) raw cashews

DIRECTIONS

1. Heat the olive oil in a large stockpot over medium heat and add in the garlic and onion. Sauté for 2–3 minutes.

2. Add the curry paste, turmeric, salt and coconut sugar and continue to sauté for another minute, then add the sweet potatoes, coconut milk and vegetable broth. Simmer for 15–20 minutes, stirring occasionally.

3. Remove the pot from the heat and allow the mixture to cool for 10–15 minutes before transferring it to a high-speed blender. Blend on high for 30 seconds, or until the mixture is smooth and there are no chunks of sweet potatoes left.

4. Transfer the mixture back to the stockpot over medium heat. Add the kale, peppers and cashews and heat for 15–20 minutes before serving.

Tip Depending on the size of your blender, you may need to blend the soup in 2–3 separate batches to prevent it from overflowing.

Game Day Bison *and* Sweet Potato Chili

Nothing screams "Game Day" like a big bowl of hearty chili in the crisp, fall weather. This flavorful twist on an autumn classic uses bison and sweet potatoes for a lean but filling combo. And the best part is, there is little prep work for this meal. Just throw the ingredients into a crockpot and let it work its magic!

Yield: 6–8 servings

Ingredients

1 lb (450 g) ground bison

1 (28-oz [794-g]) can whole peeled tomatoes

1 (14-oz [411-g]) can diced tomatoes

1 (6-oz [170-g]) can tomato paste

2 small sweet potatoes, cubed

½ cup (63 g) red pepper, finely chopped

½ cup (63 g) green pepper, finely chopped

1 cup (100 g) yellow onion, finely chopped

2 tsp (6 g) garlic, minced

2 tbsp (8 g) chili powder

1 tsp cumin

1 tsp pepper

½ tsp salt

Toppings (optional)

1 avocado, sliced

Cheese

Directions

1. Brown the bison in a skillet over medium heat, about 6–8 minutes.

2. Add all the ingredients to a crockpot and stir to combine.

3. Cook on high for 4–6 hours, or low for 10–12 hours, stirring occasionally.

4. Top with avocado slices or a sprinkle of cheese before serving (optional).

Tip The tomatoes will break down a bit on their own while cooking, but if you prefer to break them down further, try pulsing them in a food processor before adding them to the crock pot.

Spicy "Peanut" Zucchini Noodles

I don't know which part of this dish I love more—the colors or the taste! This is another one-pan meal that makes dinner prep easy and cleanup even easier. The slight spice from the "peanut" sauce brings an invigorating flavor to this already fresh and vibrant Thai-style meal.

YIELD: 4 SERVINGS

INGREDIENTS

3 large zucchinis

1 tbsp (15 ml) olive oil

1 tsp garlic, minced

1 lb (464 g) skinless, boneless chicken strips

Salt and pepper to taste

1 cup (125 g) yellow pepper

1 cup (80 g) shredded carrots

½ cup (38 g) green onion, chopped

1 cup (245 g) Spicy "Peanut" Sauce (page 170)

Cilantro, to garnish

DIRECTIONS

1. Spiralize the zucchinis into thin, spaghetti-like noodles and set aside.

2. Heat the olive oil and garlic in a large skillet over medium heat. Then add in the chicken and season with salt and pepper. Cook for 2–3 minutes per side.

3. Add the pepper, carrots and green onion to the skillet and sauté for 2–3 minutes.

4. Add the zucchini noodles and continue to sauté until the noodles are al dente, about 4–6 minutes, or done to your liking.

5. Remove from the heat and mix in the Spicy "Peanut" Sauce. Garnish with cilantro.

Tip If you don't have zucchini on hand, try pairing this meal with the Coconut Cauliflower Rice on page 87 for a more "Stir-Fry-esque" meal!

NANNY'S SPAGHETTI SAUCE *and* MEATBALLS

My Nanny made the *best* meatballs and spaghetti sauce, and it was a major staple in our house growing up. I've lightened up her meatball recipe with a few simple swaps, but her delicious sauce recipe can never be touched! Pair with veggie noodles or spaghetti squash for a healthier, classic Italian feel.

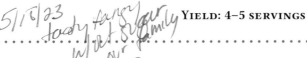

YIELD: 4–5 SERVINGS

INGREDIENTS

For the Sauce

1 tbsp (15ml) olive oil

1 tsp garlic, minced

2 (15-oz [425-g]) cans tomato sauce

4 (6-oz [170-g]) cans tomato paste

3 cups (720 ml) water

1 tsp sea salt

1 tsp dried oregano

1 cup (16 g) fresh basil, roughly chopped

For the Meatballs

1 lb (454-g) ground turkey

1 large egg, beaten

1 tsp garlic, minced

¼ cup (25 g) yellow onion, chopped

¼ cup (4 g) fresh parsley, finely chopped

¼ cup (60 g) nutritional yeast

½ tsp sea salt

½ tsp black pepper

DIRECTIONS

Preheat the oven to 350°F (176°C).

1. For the sauce, heat the oil and garlic over medium heat in a large stockpot. Add the tomato sauce, tomato paste, water, seasonings and herbs. Bring to a boil, then turn the heat to low.

2. For the meatballs, combine all of the ingredients in a large bowl and gently mix together with your hands.

3. Roll the turkey mixture into balls (about the size of a golf ball) and place them on a baking sheet lined with parchment paper.

4. Bake the meatballs for 15–20 minutes, then remove them from the oven and add to the sauce. Allow the sauce and meatballs to cook for at least one hour before serving (the longer, the better!).

> **Tip** This is a great meal to cook a in double batch. You can easily freeze both the sauce and the meatballs in an airtight container, then just thaw and re-heat for a quick, easy meal during a busy week!

Hawaiian Beef Burgers *with* Pineapple *and* Avocado

These juicy burgers will make the perfect addition to your summer barbecue menu. With their tangy flavor and sweet seasonal toppings, every bite will have your taste buds coming back for more!

YIELD: 4 BURGERS

INGREDIENTS

1 lb (454 g) ground beef

1 large egg, whisked

3 tbsp (45 ml) coconut aminos

1 tbsp (21 g) honey

1 tsp Sriracha

¼ cup (16 g) green onion, finely chopped

1 tsp garlic, minced

¼ tsp fresh ginger, grated

½ tsp sea salt

¼ tsp black pepper

1 tbsp (15 ml) olive oil

Toppings (optional)

1 avocado, sliced

4 pineapple slices

Lettuce

Tomato slices

Onion

DIRECTIONS

1. Combine the beef, egg, coconut aminos, honey, Sriracha, green onion, garlic, ginger, salt and pepper in a large bowl and gently mix together using your hands.

2. Divide the mixture into 4 even parts, and roll each into a ball using your hands. Press each into a 4-inch (10-cm) wide, ½-inch (1.3-cm) thick patty.

3. Brush the burgers with olive oil and grill over medium heat, about 3 minutes on the first side and 4 minutes on the second for medium rare, or longer to your desired degree of doneness.

4. Top the burgers with sliced avocado, pineapple and other toppings as desired.

BALSAMIC, DATE *and* PROSCIUTTO PIZZA *with* GOAT CHEESE *and* ARUGULA

This is one of my favorite recipes in this book hands-down. It combines so many of my favorite ingredients, and they all pair so perfectly together to create a super unique, delicious flavor. From the sweetness of the dates to the acidity of the balsamic vinegar, your taste buds are in for a wild (but totally awesome) ride!

YIELD: 4–5 SERVINGS

yum topping on reg crust! 4/1/23

INGREDIENTS

1 tbsp (15 ml) olive oil

1 cup (100 g) red onion, thinly sliced

½ tbsp (8 ml) balsamic vinegar

4 large medjool dates, finely chopped

3 slices prosciutto

1 All Purpose Pizza Crust (page 174)

4 oz (113 g) goat cheese, optional

Salt and pepper to taste

Arugula for topping

DIRECTIONS

Preheat the oven to 350°F (176°C).

1. In a medium skillet, heat the olive oil and add in the red onion. Sauté for 2–3 minutes, then add the balsamic vinegar and continue to sauté for an additional 2–3 minutes (the onions should be translucent and tender). Remove the skillet from the heat.

2. Arrange the onions, dates and prosciutto evenly on the pizza crust on top of a large baking sheet. Crumble the goat cheese (optional) over the top and sprinkle with salt and pepper.

3. Bake the pizza for 10–12 minutes, or until the cheese has melted.

4. Remove the pizza from the oven and top with arugula before serving.

Tip The listed amounts for each topping above is only a guideline–everyone likes their pizza a little differently, so feel free to adjust as needed!

MAPLE *Dijon* SALMON

I like to keep things simple when it comes to seafood, and this quick recipe helps me do just that. I love its sweet and tangy flavor and it pairs great with a side of grilled veggies for a light, nutritious meal.

YIELD: 4 SERVINGS

INGREDIENTS

1½ tbsp (23 g) Dijon mustard

½ tbsp (8 ml) maple syrup

¼ tsp sea salt

4 (¼-lb [225-g]) salmon filets

DIRECTIONS

Preheat the oven to 450°F (232°C).

1. Combine the Dijon mustard, maple syrup and salt in a small bowl to form the glaze.

2. Lightly brush a piece of foil with an oil of your choice and place it on a small baking sheet. Place the salmon filets on the foil and lightly brush the top of each with the glaze.

3. Bake the salmon for 10–15 minutes or until just cooked through and the salmon flakes easily with a fork.

Tip When buying your salmon, try to choose filets that are all of a similar size and thickness, so that they all cook evenly in the oven.

Italian SPAGHETTI SQUASH BOATS

Love Italian food, but hate the carb coma that often comes with it? Spaghetti squash to the rescue! The ground turkey and fresh basil in this dish keep it nice and light, while the squash keeps the carb count in control.

YIELD: 4 SERVINGS

9-9-23

INGREDIENTS

2 small spaghetti squash

2 tbsp (30 ml) olive oil, divided

2 tsp (6 g) garlic, minced

½ cup (50 g) yellow onion, diced

1 lb (464 g) mild Italian ground turkey

1 (28-oz [793-g]) can diced tomatoes

2 tbsp (2 g) fresh basil, finely chopped

Salt and pepper to taste

2 oz (57 g) fresh mozzarella cheese, optional

DIRECTIONS

Preheat the oven to 400°F (204°C).

1. Cut each squash in half, lengthwise, and scoop out the seeds. Use 1 tablespoon (15 ml) of olive oil to lightly brush the inside of each half. Place face down on a baking sheet and bake for 15 minutes, or until a sharp knife slides easily into the back.

2. While the squash is cooking, heat the remaining 1 tablespoon (15 ml) of olive oil in a skillet over medium heat and add the garlic, onions and turkey. Cook for about 6–7 minutes, or until the turkey is browned. Add the tomatoes, basil, salt and pepper and continue to cook for 2–3 minutes.

3. Drain the tomato mixture to remove excess liquid.

4. When the squash are done, flip each over and, using a fork, gently scrape out some of the strings. Fill each with the meat sauce.

5. If adding the cheese, top the boats with mozzarella and return them to the oven for 10 minutes or until the cheese has melted.

> **Tip** It's not necessary to keep the squash in "boat" form—feel free to remove the strings from the squash completely before serving if that's more your style!

* I used leftover sausage, diced. + homemade tomato sauce.

Asian Chicken Lettuce Wraps

Lettuce wraps have always been one of my go-tos at Asian restaurants, and this version is no exception! The coconut aminos gives the dish a salty, yet sweet flavor and the crunch from the lettuce gives you a crisp freshness with every bite.

YIELD: 4–5 SERVINGS

INGREDIENTS

1 lb (454 g) ground chicken

½ cup (120 ml) coconut aminos, divided

½ tsp sea salt

½ tsp black pepper

1 tbsp (15 ml) olive oil

1 tsp garlic, minced

1 cup (80 g) mushrooms, finely chopped

½ cup (50 g) yellow onion, finely chopped

¼ cup (16 g) green onion, finely chopped

½ cup (63 g) red pepper, finely chopped

½ cup (63 g) green pepper, finely chopped

¼ cup (4 g) fresh basil, finely chopped

1 head of lettuce, separated

Coconut Cauliflower Rice (page 87), optional

DIRECTIONS

1. Brown the chicken in a large skillet over medium heat with ¼ cup (60 ml) coconut aminos, salt and pepper, about 5–7 minutes. Remove the chicken from the skillet and set aside.

2. In the same skillet, heat the olive oil and garlic. Then add the mushrooms, onions and peppers and sauté for 5–7 minutes, or until tender.

3. Add the chicken back into the skillet to finish cooking, about 2–3 minutes.

4. Add the remaining coconut aminos and fresh basil.

5. Fill the lettuce cups with the chicken mixture and serve with Coconut Cauliflower Rice (optional).

Tip You can switch things up and use any kind of greens you'd like as the "wrap." Try collard greens, dino kale or swiss chard for an extra nutrient boost.

SUMMER ZUCCHINI NOODLES *with* CANTALOUPE, TURKEY SAUSAGE *and* LEMON SAUCE

We made a dish similar to this one on a family beach vacation years ago, and it always brings me back to my love of cookouts and garden-fresh summer ingredients. The sweet cantaloupe and tangy lemon sauce are so light and refreshing, and the basil gives the dish a perfect finish.

YIELD: 4–6 SERVINGS

6-2-23

INGREDIENTS

3 large zucchini

1 tbsp (15 ml) olive oil

1 lb (454 g) Italian-style ground turkey

2 ½ cups (325 g) cantaloupe, diced

2 cups (60 g) spinach

¼ cup (4 g) fresh basil, roughly chopped

½ cup (120 ml) full-fat, canned coconut milk

2 tbsp (30 m) lemon juice

Salt and pepper to taste

DIRECTIONS

1. Spiralize the zucchini into thin, spaghetti-like noodles and set aside.

2. Heat the olive oil in a large skillet and add in the turkey. Using a spatula, crumble and brown the turkey, cooking for about 3–4 minutes, then set aside.

3. In the same skillet, add the cantaloupe and sauté for about 5 minutes, then add in the zucchini noodles and spinach and continue to cook for an additional 3–5 minutes.

4. Add the turkey back into the skillet along with the basil.

5. Add the coconut milk and lemon juice and mix well to combine. Season with salt and pepper.

three

NO SWEAT SALADS, STARTERS AND SIDES

The main event is nothing without its supporting cast, and these salads, appetizers and side dishes can help jazz up any entrée. If your get-togethers with family and friends are anything like mine, they usually involve a variety of tasty food choices aside from the main course, so this chapter gives you plenty of options for your next holiday or dinner party. The Loaded Sweet Potato Skins with Bacon and Cheddar (page 72) and Spicy Almond Butter Brussels Sprouts (page 92) are two famous fan favorites!

POMEGRANATE, PEAR *and* WALNUT KALE SALAD

This salad just screams "holiday" to me, probably because it's been a staple at our family's Thanksgiving dinners for the past several years. The pomegranate and pear make this starter crisp, light and festive, and add a gorgeous pop of color to any table setting!

YIELD: 4 SERVINGS

INGREDIENTS

6 cups (120 g) kale, roughly chopped

¼ cup (42 g) pomegranate seeds

1 pear, sliced

¼ cup (30 g) walnuts, roughly chopped

Honey Dijon Vinaigrette (page 177)

DIRECTIONS

1. Toss all the ingredients (except the vinaigrette) in a large bowl.

2. Dress with Honey Dijon Vinaigrette just before serving.

Tip Wait to cut the pears until just before serving to prevent them from browning.

LOADED SWEET POTATO SKINS *with* BACON *and* CHEDDAR

If we're being honest, this tasty appetizer is really a healthy hybrid between potato skins and twice-baked potatoes, because come on, why should anyone have to choose? The creamy coconut milk and fresh garlic blended with baked sweet potato gives the filling something extra special, and topping each one off with a sprinkle of bacon and chives adds even more color and flavor to this already tasty appetizer or side dish.

YIELD: 8 POTATO SKINS

INGREDIENTS

4 medium sweet potatoes

3 strips bacon

1 tbsp (15 ml) olive oil

¼ cup (60 ml) full-fat, canned coconut milk

1 tsp garlic, minced

1 tsp sea salt

Pepper to taste

4 oz (113 g) white cheddar cheese, optional

Chives to garnish

DIRECTIONS

Preheat the oven to 400°F (204°C).

1. Pierce each sweet potato 4–5 times using a fork and place them on a baking sheet. Bake for 40–45 minutes or until the potatoes are soft.

2. While the potatoes are baking, cook the bacon in a large skillet over medium heat about 2–3 minutes per side, or until crispy. Set aside.

3. Cut each sweet potato in half, scoop out the flesh and place it in a medium bowl. Place the skins, flesh side down, back onto the baking sheet and drizzle with olive oil. Return to the oven for 6–8 minutes, or until just slightly crispy.

4. Add the coconut milk, garlic, salt and pepper to the sweet potato flesh and mash with a fork to combine. Fill each skin with the sweet potato mixture. Turn the oven down to 375°F (190°C).

5. Top each potato skin with white cheddar (if desired) and return to the oven for 10–15 minutes or until the cheese is melted. Sprinkle bacon over top and garnish with chives before serving.

Tip This recipe works great as a side dish with a protein and vegetable or for a game day appetizer to share with friends.

Crispy Chicken Tenders

Say goodbye to fast food chicken and hello to your new favorite snack! The almond and flaxseed meal coating creates a crispy outer layer while the chicken stays soft and tender inside. Pair with Two Ingredient Honey Mustard Sauce for some extra zing!

YIELD: 8 TENDERS

3/28/23

tasty

INGREDIENTS

½ cup (56 g) almond meal

2 tbsp (13 g) flaxseed meal

1 tsp garlic powder

½ tsp sea salt

½ tsp black pepper

½ tsp cayenne pepper

1 lb (454 g) boneless, skinless chicken strips

1 large egg, whisked

Two Ingredient Honey Mustard Sauce (page 178)

DIRECTIONS

Preheat the oven to 375°F (190°C).

1. Combine the almond meal, flaxseed meal and spices in a small bowl.

2. Dip each chicken strip fully into the egg to lightly coat.

3. Transfer the chicken to the almond meal mixture to lightly coat, then place on a large baking sheet covered in foil.

4. Bake for 12 minutes, flip, then bake for another 10–12 minutes until crispy.

5. Serve with Two Ingredient Honey Mustard Sauce.

Tip To make these kid-friendly or just more "bite-sized," cut each chicken strip into 2–3 pieces before coating with the egg and almond meal mixture.

Sriracha
CAULIFLOWER POPPERS

This lip-smacking, bite-sized snack packs a spicy punch, so it's great for those who can handle a little heat! The simplicity of the cauliflower really takes on the hot Sriracha flavors to bring you a fun, pop-able snack with a hit of fiber and extra nutrients!

YIELD: 4 SERVINGS

5/8/23 ok/good
a bit heavy on sauce
not crispy + spray
foil first!

INGREDIENTS
1 large head of cauliflower
¾ cup (84 g) almond meal
½ tsp sea salt
¼ tsp garlic powder
¼ tsp onion powder
½ cup (120 ml) water
½ cup (120 ml) Sriracha
1 tsp olive oil

DIRECTIONS
Preheat the oven to 450°F (232°C).

1. Cut the cauliflower into small florets.

2. In a small bowl, combine the almond meal and seasonings with the water to form a batter.

3. Dip the florets into the batter to lightly coat, then place them onto a large baking sheet covered with foil and bake for 20 minutes, flipping halfway through.

4. While the cauliflower is cooking, combine the sriracha and olive oil. Remove the cauliflower from the oven and lightly brush each piece with the Sriracha mixture.

5. Return the cauliflower to the oven for 10–12 minutes.

Tip The smaller the florets, the more these bites crisp up. I suggest cutting a few of the larger pieces into two or three smaller ones to really achieve the "breading"-like texture.

DILL *and* DIJON DEVILED EGGS

Deviled eggs are always a crowd favorite, but the fresh dill and Dijon combo in this version really takes these to the next level. You'll wow your guests with this sophisticated take on a simple classic, and the power combo of protein and healthy fats make this a lasting snack!

YIELD: 24 SERVINGS

4/9/23
not a fan

INGREDIENTS

12 large eggs

2 tbsp (30 ml) olive oil

2 tbsp (30 g) Dijon mustard

¼ cup (60 ml) water

1 tbsp (1 g) fresh dill (plus more for garnish)

½ tsp sea salt

Pepper to taste

DIRECTIONS

1. Place the eggs in a large saucepan and fill the pan with water, about 1 inch (2.5 cm) above the eggs. Bring the water to a boil over medium-high heat, about 15 minutes.

2. Cover the pan and remove from the heat. Set aside for 5 minutes, then drain the hot water and cover the eggs again with cold water. Allow the eggs to cool for about 10 minutes.

3. One by one, gently crack the shells and peel them off the eggs. Then cut each egg in half lengthwise and scoop out the yolks.

4. In a small bowl, combine the egg yolks, olive oil, mustard and water and mix together until smooth. Add the dill, salt and pepper and mix again to incorporate.

5. Refill each egg with the yolk mixture and garnish with more dill.

> **Tip** If you're making these for a party or gathering and want to take the presentation to the next level, put the filling into a pastry bag or cut a small hole in the corner of a plastic baggie, then use it to fill the eggs.

PORK Stuffed MUSHROOMS

These glorious stuffed mushrooms are made for entertaining. They're just the right size for popping, and the fun finger-foods pack so much taste with their abundance of savory flavors, that they'll have everyone standing around the appetizer table all night long!

YIELD: 16 MUSHROOMS 8/each *4/10/23 yum!*

INGREDIENTS

1 lb (454 g) baby portabella mushrooms (about 16), caps and stems separated

2 tbsp (30 ml) olive oil

1 tbsp (15 ml) red wine vinegar

½ lb (227 g) mild Italian pork sausage

¼ cup (16 g) green onion, finely chopped

1 tsp garlic

2 oz (56 g) goat cheese, optional *yes*

2 tbsp (2 g) fresh parsley, finely chopped

½ tsp sea salt

¼ tsp black pepper

DIRECTIONS

Preheat the oven to 350°F (176°C).

1. Place the mushroom caps in a medium bowl with the olive oil and vinegar and mix to lightly coat, then set aside. Finely chop the mushroom stems.

2. In a large skillet, brown the pork for 4–6 minutes, then add the mushroom stems, green onion and garlic. Continue to cook for 2–3 minutes.

3. Add the goat cheese (optional), parsley, salt and pepper and continue to cook for an additional 2–3 minutes, or until the cheese has melted.

4. Place the mushroom caps in a baking dish and fill each with the pork mixture.

5. Bake for 30 minutes.

Tip This recipe would also work well with larger mushroom caps, they just won't be as easy to grab and go!

Cilantro Sweet Potatoes *with* Garlic Crema

This recipe is so simple, but so popular! The garlic crema and fresh cilantro keep this dish light and are the perfect complements to the crispy roasted sweet potatoes. Serve the crema drizzled over the top or on the side for dipping—you can't go wrong either way!

Yield: 4 servings

INGREDIENTS

2 medium sweet potatoes

1 tbsp (15 ml) olive oil

½ tsp sea salt

¼ tsp black pepper

For the Crema

¼ cup (60 ml) full-fat, canned coconut milk

1 tsp garlic, minced

Dash of sea salt

1 cup (16 g) chopped fresh cilantro, loosely packed

DIRECTIONS

Preheat the oven to 400°F (204°C).

1. Cut the sweet potatoes into 1–2 inch (2.5–5 cm) wedges.

2. In a large bowl, combine the sweet potatoes, olive oil, salt and pepper and mix until the sweet potatoes are evenly coated.

3. Place the sweet potatoes in an even layer on a baking sheet lined with parchment paper and cook for 25 minutes.

4. While the sweet potatoes are cooking, combine all of the crema ingredients in a small bowl.

5. Remove the sweet potatoes from the oven, drizzle with the crema and sprinkle with cilantro.

Garlicky Parsnip Fries

These fries are sure to become a staple in your house on burger night. The parsnips make for a great side to any meal, and the garlic flavor will rock your world with every crispy bite!

Yield: 4 servings *3/7/23 Tasty.*

INGREDIENTS

3 large parsnips

1 tbsp (15 ml) olive oil

½ tsp sea salt

1 tsp garlic, minced

DIRECTIONS

Preheat the oven to 375°F (190°C).

1. Roughly peel the parsnips and slice them into thin strips (⅛ inch [.3 cm] thick).

2. In a large bowl, combine the parsnips with the olive oil, salt and garlic until they are evenly coated.

3. Spread the parsnips into one layer on a baking sheet lined with parchment paper, making sure that none overlap.

4. Bake for 40–45 minutes, flipping halfway through. Remove from the oven when the fries have become slightly crispy.

Tip When slicing parsnips, first cut them in half horizontally, then vertically to make them easier to manage. The thinner you slice the pieces, the crispier they will get!

Coconut CAULIFLOWER RICE

Cauliflower rice is probably one of the most versatile sides there is. Just like regular rice, it can take on the flavor profiles of any meal, but it can also give you that "bulk" you're looking for without extra calories or carbohydrates. This version is meant to act as a blank canvas—feel free to use it as is or add whatever spices or herbs you feel fit for any meal you pair it with. For example, add a little cilantro and mix it into the Mexican Fiesta Skillet (page 45) or add some coconut aminos and use it as a base for the Easy Chicken Vegetable Stir-Fry (page 46). Don't be afraid to get creative!

YIELD: 4 SERVINGS

2/2/23
tasty

INGREDIENTS

1 medium head of cauliflower

2 tbsp (28 g) coconut oil

1 tsp garlic, minced

¼ cup (60 ml) full-fat, canned coconut milk

1 tsp sea salt

Pepper to taste

DIRECTIONS

1. Chop the cauliflower into small florets.

2. Place the florets into a food processor and pulse on low until broken down into "rice" size pieces, about 10 seconds. (Depending on the size of your food processor, you may need to do this in 2–3 separate batches).

3. Heat the coconut oil and garlic in a skillet over medium heat. Add in the cauliflower and sauté for 2–3 minutes.

4. Add the coconut milk, salt and pepper and continue to sauté until the cauliflower becomes soft in consistency, or "rice-like," about 5–7 minutes.

Tip Make a big batch at the beginning of the week and season a portioned amount each evening to complement your daily dinner plans!

PROSCIUTTO *Wrapped* ASPARAGUS SPEARS

Roasted asparagus is great on its own, but prosciutto adds a little extra flavor and crispness to this ever-popular side dish.

YIELD: 4–5 SERVINGS

yum! 1-28-23

INGREDIENTS

30–35 asparagus spears, trimmed (thin is best)

1 tbsp (15 ml) olive oil

½ tsp sea salt

Pepper to taste

5 oz (140 g) prosciutto, separated into slices about 2 inches (5 cm) long

DIRECTIONS

Preheat the oven to 350°F (176°C).

1. In a large bowl, combine the asparagus, olive oil, salt and pepper and toss to evenly coat the asparagus.

2. Wrap 1 slice of prosciutto tightly around 4–5 asparagus spears and place directly onto a baking sheet.

3. Bake for 10 minutes, then place the baking sheet under the broiler for 1 minute or until the prosciutto is slightly crispy.

Tip Prosciutto is delicate, so it can be difficult to work with. But don't worry about each slice being perfect or identical, just make sure each piece is long enough to wrap with!

Colorful PINEAPPLE SLAW

This colorful side adds a little crunch to burgers or tacos, and its fresh, tangy flavors from lime and coconut keep it light and refreshing!

YIELD: 6–8 SERVINGS

halve this?

INGREDIENTS

4 cups (275 g) green cabbage, roughly chopped and loosely packed

3 cups (200 g) red cabbage, roughly chopped and loosely packed

2 cups (300 g) pineapple, diced

½ cup (50 g) red onion, finely chopped

¼ cup (60 ml) full-fat, canned coconut milk

2 tbsp (30 ml) lime juice

2 tbsp (30 ml) apple cider vinegar

1 tsp coconut sugar *sub*

1 tsp sea salt

Pepper to taste

¼ cup (4 g) cilantro, finely chopped

DIRECTIONS

1. In a large bowl, toss together the cabbage, pineapple and red onion.

2. In a small bowl, combine the coconut milk, lime juice, apple cider vinegar, coconut sugar, salt and pepper.

3. Pour the coconut milk mixture over the slaw and add the cilantro. Toss again to evenly coat.

4. Cover the slaw and refrigerate for several hours before serving for the best flavor.

> **Tip** Some of the juices in this dish will settle at the bottom while refrigerating. Be sure to toss the slaw again before serving to distribute the flavors evenly.

Spicy Almond Butter Brussels Sprouts

Savory, sweet, spicy—there's a little something for everyone in this side dish! My friend, Sarah (a fellow dietitian!), and I served these as a side at a charity dinner event we hosted over the holiday season, and they were the star of the three course meal. We had so many people tell us that this recipe changed their minds about Brussels sprouts! The sweet and savory combo makes these a major crowd pleaser!

YIELD: 4 SERVINGS

INGREDIENTS

2 tbsp (30 ml) olive oil

½ cup (64 g) almond butter

1 tbsp (21 g) honey

1 tbsp (15 ml) Sriracha

Splash of lemon juice

½ tsp sea salt

Pepper to taste

1 lb (680 g) Brussels sprouts, halved

DIRECTIONS

Preheat the oven to 375°F (190°C).

1. Combine the olive oil, almond butter, honey, Sriracha, lemon juice, salt and pepper in a large bowl.

2. Add the Brussels sprouts to the bowl and mix with the sauce to evenly coat.

3. Spread the Brussels sprouts evenly in one layer on a large baking sheet.

4. Bake for 20 minutes, tossing halfway through.

341 cal

Tip If small leaves fall off of the Brussels sprouts as you are cutting or mixing them, don't throw them away! Throw them on to the baking sheet instead for a few crispier bites.

Rosemary Roasted Red Potatoes

This one's for all of my meat and potatoes guys (and girls!) out there. The rosemary takes this simple roasted veggie recipe to the next level and makes a great side for any dinner.

YIELD: 4 SERVINGS

INGREDIENTS

2 lbs (907 g) baby red potatoes, quartered

1 tbsp (15 ml) olive oil

1 tsp garlic, minced

½ tsp sea salt

Pepper to taste

4–5 rosemary sprigs

DIRECTIONS

Preheat the oven to 475°F (246°C).

1. Combine the potatoes, olive oil, garlic, salt and pepper in a large bowl and mix to evenly coat the potatoes.

2. Transfer the potatoes to a baking dish and lay the rosemary sprigs on top.

3. Bake for 30 minutes, tossing halfway through, or until potatoes are tender.

four

JUST FOR ONE (OR TWO)

One of the most common barriers I see with nutrition clients is that they often find it difficult and unmotivating to cook for just one or two people. So I included this chapter to offer a few recipes that have serving sizes and ingredient lists tailored for just that. Try the Tropical Green Smoothie Bowl (page 99) for a quick, single-serve breakfast and the Pesto Chicken and Summer Veggie Packets (page 104) for a healthy dinner for two.

Tropical Green Smoothie Bowl

The mango and pineapple in this smoothie make it the ultimate energizing breakfast, and adding it to a bowl makes it feel a bit more like a "real" meal for me. Top it with a little Everyday Granola (page 117) and you've got yourself a refreshing and satisfying morning meal!

YIELD: 1 SMOOTHIE

INGREDIENTS

1 cup (240 ml) unsweetened almond milk

1 large banana

½ cup (70 g) frozen pineapple

½ cup (70 g) frozen mango

1 tbsp (16 g) almond butter

1 tbsp (7 g) ground flax meal

2–3 large handfuls of spinach

6–7 ice cubes

DIRECTIONS

1. Combine all the ingredients in a high-speed blender and blend until smooth, about 30–45 seconds.

Tip If you only like pineapple or only like mango, you can use 1 full cup (140 g) of your desired choice and omit the other for a similarly refreshing taste.

Easy Onion, Kale *and* Sweet Potato Omelet

I call this omelet my go-to "lazy girl" meal, as I find myself eating it when I don't have time to make anything extravagant or time-consuming (which is often!). Who says omelets are only for breakfast? The veggies in this one make for a hearty, savory meal at any time of the day AND it gives you a great blend of protein, healthy fats and carbs, which, being a dietitian, I am a big fan of!

Yield: 1 omelet

3/4/23 .... good

Ingredients

1 tbsp (15 ml) melted coconut oil

½ small sweet potato, cut into small cubes

¼ cup (25 g) yellow onion, roughly chopped

½ cup (10 g) roughly chopped kale _spin._

3 large eggs

3 tbsp (45 ml) unsweetened almond milk _coc._

Salt and pepper to taste

Directions

1. Melt the coconut oil in a small skillet over medium heat and add the sweet potatoes and onion. Sauté until the sweet potatoes begin to soften and the onions become translucent, about 5–7 minutes, then add in the kale and continue to sauté until it begins to wilt. Remove the mixture from the skillet and set aside.

2. In a small bowl, whisk together the eggs, almond milk, salt and pepper.

3. Add the eggs to the skillet and cook until the bottom side of the omelet is firm, about 3–5 minutes.

4. Add the filling mixture so that one half of the omelet is covered. Flip the other side over top and continue to cook until the egg is fully cooked on the inside, about 3–5 minutes.

389 cal

Tip Feel free to add whatever veggies you have on hand into this recipe. I love the sweet potato, kale and onion combo, but omelets are the perfect base for using up whatever is left in your fridge from the week!

Classic CHOPPED SALAD

I love the vibrant colors and abundance of fresh ingredients in this salad and the fact that you get a little bit of everything with each bite. I once made this salad for a cooking demo, and it was a huge hit with the whole audience! It's a great option for a light lunch or quick dinner.

YIELD: 1 SALAD

INGREDIENTS

1 cup (40 g) kale, roughly chopped

½ cup (35 g) radicchio, roughly chopped

½ cup (35 g) napa cabbage, roughly chopped

2 oz (56 g) roasted turkey, cut into small pieces

1 slice bacon, crumbled

½ large avocado, cubed

2 tbsp (28 g) chopped apple

1 tbsp (14 g) raw almonds

Blue cheese crumbles, optional

Honey Dijon Vinaigrette (page 177)

DIRECTIONS

1. Assemble a base of kale, radicchio and cabbage, then add the remaining ingredients (except the vinaigrette) over the top.

2. Lightly dress with Honey Dijon Vinaigrette.

Pesto Chicken *and* Summer Veggie Packets

If you're looking for a no-hassle meal for two, then this lean summer dinner is the answer to your prayers! All you have to do is combine the ingredients in the foil, wrap them up and bake. When the oven dings, you've got a gorgeous summer dinner for you and your guest, and, even better, no mess to clean up!

YIELD: 2 SERVINGS

INGREDIENTS

1 tbsp (15 ml) olive oil

2 (4 oz [113 g]) boneless, skinless chicken breasts

2 tbsp (30 g) Homemade Basil Pesto (page 166)

½ small zucchini, thinly sliced

¼ cup (16 g) green onions, finely chopped

¼ cup (40 g) tomato, diced

Salt and pepper to taste

DIRECTIONS

Preheat the oven to 350°F (176°C).

1. Lay out two pieces of foil large enough to assemble and wrap all the ingredients. Drizzle ½ tablespoon (8 ml) olive oil in the middle of each and place 1 chicken breast on top.

2. Spread 1 tablespoon (15 g) of pesto onto each chicken breast, then evenly divide the zucchini, green onion, and tomato and assemble on top of each piece.

3. One piece at a time, lift the sides of the foil and bring them together over the top of the chicken to secure shut. Place both packets on a baking sheet.

4. Bake for 30 minutes. Remove the packets from the oven and unfold the foil to serve.

> **Tip** Try your best to buy 2 chicken breasts that are equal in size and thickness to ensure even cooking in the oven.

Creamy Avocado Pudding

This is one of my all time *favorite* nighttime snacks when I have a sweet tooth attack. The sweetness from the small amount of honey is just enough to curb any sugar craving, and the creaminess from the sunflower seed butter and avocado give this pudding a smooth, fudgy flavor. This recipe makes two servings, but it will be easy to convince yourself it's just one!

YIELD: 1–2 SERVINGS

INGREDIENTS

1 small avocado, skin removed and pitted, mashed

2 tbsp (32 g) almond butter

1 tbsp (15 g) honey

2 tbsp (30 ml) unsweetened almond milk

2 tbsp (10 g) unsweetened cocoa powder

Dash of vanilla extract

½ tsp sea salt

Cacao nibs, optional

DIRECTIONS

1. Combine all the ingredients in a small bowl and mash with a fork until all are well combined and the mixture is smooth.

2. Stir in the cacao nibs (optional).

Tip This pudding can also be made in a high speed blender for a smoother texture if desired.

APPLE CRISP *for Two*

This yummy treat is about as close to apple pie as you can get (minus the sugar overload!). The apple and cinnamon combo has always been a classic, but the almond butter crumble adds a sweet richness that takes this miniature version to the next level.

YIELD: 2 SERVINGS

. . . .

INGREDIENTS

1 small apple, cored and thinly sliced

1 tbsp (15 ml) coconut oil, melted

½ tsp ground cinnamon

¼ cup (28 g) almond meal

2 tbsp (32 g) almond butter

½ tsp honey

½ tsp vanilla extract

Pinch sea salt

DIRECTIONS

Preheat oven to 350°F (176°C).

1. In a small bowl, combine the apple slices with the coconut oil and cinnamon. Layer the apple slices evenly in the bottom of 2 small tart dishes or ramekins.

2. In another bowl, combine the almond meal, almond butter, honey, vanilla extract and salt. Mix until crumbly in texture.

3. Crumble the almond meal mixture evenly over each dish.

4. Place both dishes on a small baking sheet and bake for 10 minutes.

Tip I love this treat with apples, but feel free to use any fruit you'd like to switch things up or to use what's in season. Peaches or bananas make great substitutes!

five

SIMPLE SNACKS

Whether you're at home, at a party or on-the-go, healthy snacks are a great way to help hold you over in-between meals and are a great opportunity for fitting in some extra nutrients throughout your day! From muffins and snack bites to guacamole and salsa, this chapter has something to fit your snacking needs at any time and keep you powering through your day!

Dark Chocolate Pecan Snack Bites

I love this sweet and salty combo for a quick snack on-the-run or for a guilt-free sweet bite after lunch or dinner. The fiber from the dates and healthy fats from the pecans make these a great balanced snack, with nutrients galore. Plus, the bite-sized shape makes portion control easy!

YIELD: 12–15 BITES

INGREDIENTS

1 cup (120 g) raw pecans

1 cup (150 g) medjool dates, pitted

¼ cup (84 g) honey

¼ cup (53 g) mini dark chocolate chips

DIRECTIONS

1. Combine the pecans and dates in a food processor and pulse on high for 30–60 seconds or until the dates are broken down.

2. Add the honey and pulse on low for 15–20 seconds or until the mixture starts to pull away from the sides of the bowl.

3. Stir in the chocolate chips.

4. Using your hands, roll the mixture into small balls, about 1 inch (2.5 cm) in diameter.

Tip The bites may feel a bit greasy when you're rolling them. But not to worry—it's just the healthy oils coming out from the pecans!

Maple Vanilla Chia Seed Pudding

I was always a big fan of pudding as a kid, but I'm now an even bigger fan as an adult thanks to this recipe. The chia seeds bring superfood powers to this recipe, and I love swirling in a spoonful of nut butter and a handful of frozen blueberries for a dreamy morning treat!

Yield: 4 servings

Ingredients

½ cup (96 g) chia seeds

2 cups (480 ml) unsweetened almond milk

1 tbsp (15 ml) maple syrup

1 tsp vanilla extract

Toppings (optional)

Nut butter

Berries

Everyday Granola (page 117)

Directions

1. Combine all the ingredients in a large bowl.

2. Whisk the mixture for 1 minute, making sure that there are no clumps of chia seeds left.

3. Refrigerate for at least 2 hours to thicken before serving, stirring occasionally.

4. Top with nut butter, berries and Everyday Granola as desired.

Tip Adjust the amount of maple syrup to your liking—using more or less depending on how sweet you want it. You can also try subbing a few drops of stevia if you want to keep the recipe completely sugar-free!

Everyday GRANOLA

This recipe may win the award for the one in this book that I make the most often. I love granola but don't always love the unnecessary ingredients that come in most packaged varieties. I'm obsessed with this sweet and crunchy combo and love using it to top smoothie bowls and chia pudding, or just pouring some almond milk over a little bowl for a healthy bedtime snack.

YIELD: 4–5 SERVINGS

12-17-23 easy
lightly sweet/salty

INGREDIENTS

1 cup (60 g) coconut flakes

½ cup (55 g) pecans, roughly chopped

½ cup (60 g) almonds, roughly chopped

½ cup (60 g) pumpkin seeds

2 tbsp (7 g) chia seeds

¼ tsp sea salt

2 tbsp (28 g) coconut oil, melted

2 tbsp (42 g) honey

1 tsp vanilla extract

DIRECTIONS

Preheat the oven to 300°F (148°C).

1. Combine the coconut flakes, nuts, seeds and salt in a large bowl.

2. Add the coconut oil, honey and vanilla and mix until the nuts and seeds are evenly coated.

3. Arrange the granola in a thin layer on a large baking sheet lined with parchment paper and bake for 12–15 minutes, or until the coconut flakes turn golden brown, tossing halfway through.

Tip Sub any nuts/seeds you'd like in this recipe. I've tried multiple combinations and have yet to find one I didn't like!

Carrot Cake Muffins

Adding veggies to baked goods (and still making them taste good) is the best magic trick one can acquire in my mind. You can have your cake and eat it, too, with these perfectly healthy muffins. Carrots have a natural sweetness that help them blend in easily with the other ingredients in this recipe, and you'll feel like you're indulging every time you take a bite.

Yield: 10 muffins

Ingredients

2 large bananas, mashed
(about 1 cup [200 g])

2 large eggs

¼ cup (84 g) honey

¼ cup (64 g) almond butter

1 cup (100 g) finely shredded carrots

¼ cup (28 g) coconut flour

1 tsp baking soda

1 tsp cinnamon

¼ tsp cardamom

¼ tsp ground ginger

¼ tsp sea salt

Directions

Preheat the oven to 350°F (176°C).

1. Combine the bananas, eggs, honey, almond butter and carrots in a large mixing bowl.

2. In a separate bowl, combine the coconut flour, baking soda, spices and salt.

3. Add the dry ingredients to the wet and mix well until a batter forms.

4. Pour the batter evenly into a muffin tin lined with paper or silicon liners, filling each to the top.

5. Bake for 20 minutes or until a toothpick comes out clean in the center.

BANANA *Chocolate Chip* MUFFINS

These yummy muffins are adult and kid-friendly, and they make for a great breakfast or snack on-the-go! The almond butter base gives them strong staying power, with a healthy fat and protein combo that will keep you fuller than your typical muffin from the store or coffee shop. Keep one or two of these in your bag for that 3 o'clock afternoon slump at school or work and you'll have a little pep back in your step in no time!

YIELD: 10 MUFFINS

INGREDIENTS

2 large bananas, mashed

2 large eggs

1 cup (256 g) almond butter

2 tbsp (30 g) honey

1 tsp vanilla extract

1 tsp baking soda

½ tsp sea salt

¼ cup (60 g) dark chocolate chips

DIRECTIONS

Preheat the oven to 350°F (176°C).

1. Combine all the ingredients except for the chocolate chips in a large mixing bowl.

2. Stir in the chocolate chips.

3. Pour the batter evenly into a muffin tin lined with paper or silicon liners, filling each to the top.

4. Bake for 15 minutes or until a toothpick comes out clean in the center.

Tip The riper the bananas, the sweeter these will taste!

Orange CASHEW DATE BITES

I got inspiration for this recipe from a gluten-free bakery I visited a few years ago and it's been one of my favorites ever since! The flavors of the orange and cardamom combined with the dates make for a unique flavor that I love, and these bite-sized snacks are perfect for throwing into your purse or backpack on a busy day.

YIELD: 10 BITES

INGREDIENTS

1 cup (112 g) raw cashews

10 large medjool dates, halved and pitted

¼ tsp cardamom

Zest of 1 orange

2 tbsp (10 g) shredded unsweetened coconut

DIRECTIONS

1. Combine all the ingredients except for the coconut in a food processor and blend for 30 seconds, or until the mixture starts to ball up and pull away from the sides of the bowl.

2. Roll the mixture into bite-size balls (about 1 inch [2.5 cm] in diameter) then roll into the coconut to lightly coat.

Tip These could also easily be made into bars by pressing the mixture into the bottom of a loaf pan and cut into squares.

Uncle Dave's Salsa

This salsa is inspired by my Uncle Dave's recipe (I had to bribe him to let me put it in this book!). He makes it every time we visit and I swear it just gets better and better. The fresh ingredients trump store-bought versions every time, and it's so easy to blend up in the food processor. I've been known to eat it right from there without even putting it in a serving bowl—I just can't wait!

YIELD: 3 CUPS (777 G)

INGREDIENTS

2 (14.5-oz [411-g]) cans diced tomatoes

1 tbsp (15 ml) lime juice

½ tbsp (8 ml) white vinegar

¾ cup (75 g) yellow onion, diced

½ cup (8 g) fresh cilantro

2 tsp (6 g) garlic, minced

1 tsp sea salt

¾ tsp cumin

½ tsp black pepper

DIRECTIONS

1. Drain the tomatoes.

2. Add all the ingredients to a food processor and pulse 8–10 times (more or less depending on the consistency you prefer) to combine.

Tip If you like your salsa chilled like I do, let this sit in the fridge for about an hour or so before serving. It lets the flavors marinate a little more, too!

5 Minute GUACAMOLE

Guacamole is one of my all time favorite foods, and *homemade* guacamole really takes the cake for me. There's just something about the fresh, creamy avocado that makes me swoon, and the addition of the lime juice and cilantro in this version takes that freshness factor even further.

YIELD: 4–6 SERVINGS

INGREDIENTS

4 avocados, pitted, skin removed, and mashed

½ cup (150 g) tomato, diced

¼ cup (25 g) red onion, diced

2 tbsp (30 ml) fresh lime juice

2 tbsp (2 g) cilantro, finely chopped

1 garlic clove, minced

½ tsp sea salt

Pepper to taste

DIRECTIONS

1. Combine all the ingredients in a large bowl and mix together using a fork.

Tip News flash! Your guac doesn't always have to be perfectly smooth. (I know, crazy, right?) Try keeping the mashing to a minimum to create a guacamole with a creamy chunk or two in each bite!

six

"Piece of Cake" Sweets

When your sweet tooth calls and you need an easy (but healthier) fix, look no further. The grain-free treats in this chapter are always crowd-pleasers with their taste and simplicity, and they will have anyone you share them with coming back for more! If you're looking for something light and fresh, try the yummy Fruit Pizza with Coconut Cream Spread (page 143). And if you're in the mood for something rich and decadent, try the Rich Chocolate Ramekin Cakes (page 144).

ALMOND BUTTER *Swirl* BROWNIES

I've made these brownies for countless occasions, and they are always a HUGE crowd pleaser, no matter what (people just can't resist that swirl!). Plus, they're super easy to throw together when you're in a pinch. Pair one with a big glass of almond milk and you'll be in grain-free dessert heaven!

YIELD: 12 BROWNIES

3-23-23
350°   *ok/good*

INGREDIENTS

½ cup (56 g) coconut flour

½ cup (40 g) cocoa powder

½ tsp baking powder

¼ tsp sea salt

5 large eggs

½ cup (168 g) honey

¼ cup (56 g) coconut oil, melted

¼ cup (64 g) almond butter

DIRECTIONS

1. Combine the coconut flour, cocoa powder, baking powder and salt together in a small bowl.

2. In a large bowl, combine the eggs, honey and coconut oil.

3. Slowly add the dry ingredients to the wet, mixing well until a batter forms.

4. Pour the batter into an 8 x 8 inch (20 x 20 cm) (or similar) baking dish lined with parchment paper and swirl in the almond butter using a knife.

5. Bake for 20–25 minutes or until a toothpick comes out clean in the center.

even better warm

Chunky Chocolate Cookies

When it comes to cookies, I say the chunkier the better. Walnuts add a little healthy fat and crunch action to this otherwise soft and gooey treat, and they're just perfect for dunking into a big glass of almond milk!

YIELD: 12 COOKIES

INGREDIENTS

¼ cup + 1 tbsp (35 g) coconut flour

¼ cup (20 g) unsweetened cocoa powder

1 tsp baking soda

1 tsp sea salt

2 large eggs

⅓ cup (112 g) honey

¼ cup (56 g) coconut oil, melted

1 tsp vanilla

¼ cup (30 g) chopped walnuts

¼ cup (60 g) dark chocolate chips, optional

DIRECTIONS

Preheat the oven to 350°F (176°C).

1. Combine the coconut flour, cocoa powder, baking soda and salt in a medium bowl.

2. In a large bowl, combine the eggs, honey, coconut oil and vanilla.

3. Add the dry ingredients to the wet and mix until all of the ingredients are well incorporated. Stir in the walnuts and chocolate chips (optional).

4. Drop the batter by the spoonful onto a baking sheet lined with parchment paper.

5. Bake for 10–12 minutes.

AB Flax Cookies

These cookies are almost *too* easy to make. So easy that I have more than once found myself whipping up
a small batch *multiple* times per week to fight my after-dinner sweet tooth cravings. All of the ingredients are ones that
I almost always have on hand at home, and the cookies are egg-free which is a bonus for those with allergies!
I love the addition of flaxseed meal for a little extra punch of nutrients, too!

YIELD: 15 COOKIES

INGREDIENTS

2 tbsp (13 g) flaxseed meal

¼ cup + 1 tbsp (75 ml) water

¾ cup (192 g) almond butter

¼ cup (84 g) honey

1 tsp vanilla extract

¼ cup + 1 tbsp (35 g) coconut flour

1 tsp baking soda

¼ tsp sea salt

DIRECTIONS

Preheat the oven to 350°F (176°C).

1. Combine the flaxseed meal and water in a small bowl and set aside to allow a
gel to form, about 5 minutes.

2. In a large bowl, combine the flax gel, almond butter, honey and vanilla extract.

3. In a separate bowl, combine the coconut flour, baking soda and salt and slowly add
the dry ingredients to the wet to form a dough.

4. Roll the dough into balls (about 1 inch [2.5 cm] in diameter) and place them
on a cookie sheet lined with parchment paper. Using a fork, press a crisscross pattern
into each cookie.

5. Bake for 10 minutes.

Tip If you want to make these cookies completely allergy-friendly, use
sunflower seed butter in place of the almond butter!

Coconut Milk Ice Cream Four Ways

The silky smooth consistency of coconut milk makes it an absolutely excellent base for any ice cream flavor, and I love the versatility the base recipe has. Each of these flavors brings something unique to the table, so there is sure to be something for everyone!

Yield: 1 ½ cups (258 g)

Ingredients

Base Recipe

1 (14-oz [397-ml]) can full-fat coconut milk

3 tbsp (45 ml) maple syrup

1 tsp vanilla extract

½ tsp sea salt

For Mint Chocolate Chip

(Add during heating)

2 tsp (10 ml) peppermint extract

(Add during mixing)

2 tbsp (30 g) mini dark chocolate chips

For Salty Sunflower Seed Butter Swirl

(Add during mixing)

Additional ½ tsp sea salt

½ cup (64 g) sunflower seed butter

For Chocolate Almond and Coconut

(Add during heating)

2 tbsp (10 g) cocoa powder

(Add during mixing)

¼ cup (20 g) unsweetened shredded coconut

¼ cup (24 g) almonds, finely chopped

For Blackberry

(Add during mixing)

¼ cup (83 g) Blackberry Chia Jam (page 173)

Directions

1. Combine the coconut milk, maple syrup, vanilla and salt in a small saucepan over medium heat. Add in the additional ingredients if listed and stir continuously for 2–3 minutes. Remove from the heat and allow the mixture to cool in the refrigerator for at least 2 hours.

2. Pour the mixture into an ice cream maker and use as directed, adding the mix-ins about halfway through.

BUCKEYES

Growing up in Columbus, Ohio, making buckeyes was a common practice in the Riggs household on football Saturdays—which probably explains why I've always been a fan of the chocolate and peanut butter combo. This version uses almond butter and dark chocolate (an even better combo, in my mind!), but still has the same nostalgic taste that I remember from my childhood.

YIELD: 12-15 BUCKEYES

186cal each!

4/7/23 v/good

INGREDIENTS

1 cup (256 g) almond butter *natural pb*

2 tbsp (42 g) honey *omit*

1 tsp vanilla extract

1 tsp sea salt *omit*

½ cup + 1 tbsp (63 g) coconut flour

¾ cup (180 g) dark chocolate chips *semisweet*

1 tbsp (14 g) coconut oil

DIRECTIONS

1. Combine the almond butter, honey, vanilla, salt and coconut flour and mix until a dough forms.

2. Roll the dough into small balls (about 1 inch [2.5 cm] in diameter) and place the balls onto a large plate or baking sheet lined with wax paper. Refrigerate for 30–60 minutes or until very firm.

3. Once the buckeyes are firm, melt the chocolate chips and coconut oil over low heat, stirring continuously until melted completely, about 4–6 minutes. Remove from heat.

4. Using a toothpick, dip the buckeyes one at a time about ¾ of the way into the chocolate mixture, leaving a small area uncovered at the top. Place back onto the wax paper.

5. Allow the excess chocolate to drip off, then return the baking sheet to the refrigerator and allow the chocolate to harden, about 20–30 minutes minimum. Using your fingertips, cover the holes from the toothpick. Store in the refrigerator.

> **Tip** To prevent excess chocolate from forming under each candy after dipping, use your non-toothpick-holding hand to gently tap the holding hand, allowing excess chocolate to drip back into the pan before placing the candy onto the baking sheet.

Coconut Almond Bark

Bark is the treat you can take to any gathering that looks and tastes like a million bucks but is so incredibly simple to throw together. The sweet and salty mix-ins in this coconut almond variety give a little crunch with each bite!

YIELD: ABOUT 10 OZ (283 G)

INGREDIENTS

10 oz (283 g) dark chocolate

¼ cup (15 g) unsweetened coconut flakes

¼ cup (24 g) almonds, finely chopped

½ tsp sea salt

DIRECTIONS

1. Melt the chocolate in a small saucepan over low heat, continuously stirring until completely smooth, about 4–6 minutes.

2. Pour the chocolate into a thin layer over a piece of wax paper on a small baking sheet.

3. Sprinkle the coconut flakes, almonds and salt evenly over the top of the chocolate.

4. Place the baking sheet in the freezer to harden the chocolate for at least 30 minutes, then remove and break the bark into pieces using your hands or a knife. Store the bark in the freezer.

Tip To achieve a different look for this bark, you can also mix the almonds and coconut into the melted chocolate before pouring it over the wax paper.

Fruit Pizza *with* Coconut Cream Spread

Coconut cream and a sweet almond flour crust give this fun dessert a healthier twist that makes it the perfect addition to any summer party or cookout. Topped with fresh fruit, it's a treat kids (and adults) of all ages will love!

Yield: 8 servings

Ingredients

For the Crust

2 cups (224 g) almond meal

1 tsp sea salt

1 large egg

¼ cup (56 g) coconut oil, melted

1 tsp vanilla extract

For the Spread

1 cup (240 ml) coconut cream

1 tbsp (15 g) honey

Splash of vanilla extract

Toppings (optional)

Strawberries, thinly sliced

Kiwi, thinly sliced

Bananas, thinly sliced

Blueberries

Raspberries

Blackberries

Directions

Preheat the oven to 350°F (176°C).

1. Combine all the crust ingredients in a food processor or large bowl and mix to form a dough.

2. Roll the dough into a ball and then roll out between two pieces of parchment paper, about ⅙ inch (4 mm) thick. Remove the top piece of parchment and place the crust along with the bottom piece onto a baking sheet. Bake for 11–12 minutes.

3. While the crust is baking, combine the coconut cream, honey and vanilla to form the spread. Refrigerate for at least 20 minutes.

4. Remove the crust from the oven and allow it to cool completely, about 25–30 minutes.

5. Once the crust is cool, spread the coconut cream mixture evenly over it and top with fruits of your choice. Store in the refrigerator.

Tip You can now buy coconut cream on its own at the grocery store, but if you can't find it in one near you, just refrigerate one or two cans of full-fat coconut milk overnight, and use the cream that forms from it instead!

Rich Chocolate Ramekin Cakes

These ramekin cakes are so decadent, it's hard to believe they only have five ingredients!
I love making these for Valentine's Day or birthdays for a rich, chocolate indulgence!

YIELD: 3 CAKES

. . . .

INGREDIENTS

3 oz (86 g) dark chocolate

¼ cup + 1 tbsp (70 g) coconut oil

½ cup (120 ml) maple syrup

2 large eggs

1 cup (112 g) almond meal

DIRECTIONS

Preheat the oven to 350°F (176°C).

1. Combine the chocolate, coconut oil and maple syrup in a small saucepan over low heat, stirring continuously until the chocolate is completely melted, about 3–5 minutes.

2. Remove the pan from the heat.

3. Whisk the eggs together in a medium bowl and add the chocolate mixture. Add the almond meal and continue to mix until all the ingredients are well incorporated.

4. Pour the batter evenly into three 7-ounce (198-g) ramekins lightly coated with coconut oil.

5. Bake for 20 minutes and serve immediately.

Tip If you're serving these for a party or special gathering and want to add a little something to the presentation, blend a little coconut sugar in a food processor until it becomes a powder, then sprinkle a pinch or two over the top of each cake, or serve with a scoop of Coconut Milk Ice Cream (page 136).

Chocolate Peppermint Cups

The mint and chocolate combo can't be beat, and these bite-sized treats are great
for popping after dinner to refresh your palate.

YIELD: ABOUT 20 CUPS

INGREDIENTS

10 oz (283 g) dark chocolate chips

3 tbsp (42 g) coconut oil

2 tsp (10 ml) peppermint extract

DIRECTIONS

1. Combine the chocolate and coconut oil in a small saucepan over low heat, stirring continuously until the chocolate is completely melted, about 4–5 minutes.

2. Mix in the peppermint extract and remove from the heat.

3. Pour the mixture evenly into mini muffin or candy papers, filling them almost all the way to the top.

4. Place the cups in the freezer to set (at least 15 minutes). Store in the freezer.

> *Tip* If you don't have small candy or muffin papers, you can still make these with the regular-sized version. Just fill each about ⅛ inch (3 mm) high to make them easier for eating.

Soft *and* Gooey Blondie Bars

Warning: these bars are addicting. *Seriously* addicting. Sweetened naturally with only dates and banana, they'll knock any refined-sugar-sweetened dessert out of the park. I like baking them until the middle is just almost done, hence the description "soft and gooey."

Yield: 9 bars

INGREDIENTS

10 large medjool dates, pitted and halved

1 tbsp (15 ml) water, divided

1 cup (256 g) almond butter

3 large eggs

1 large banana, mashed

¼ cup (60 ml) unsweetened almond milk

1 tsp vanilla extract

1 tsp baking soda

½ tsp sea salt

DIRECTIONS

Preheat the oven to 350°F (176°C).

1. Combine the dates and ½ tablespoon (7 ml) of water in a small saucepan over medium heat for 1–2 minutes, or until the dates begin to soften. Remove the pan from the heat and add the remaining ½ tablespoon (7 ml) of water, then mash the dates into a paste (this should make about ¼ cup [61 g]).

2. Combine the date paste, almond butter, eggs, banana, almond milk and vanilla in a large bowl.

3. Add in the baking soda and salt and mix well.

4. Pour the batter evenly into an 8 x 8 inch (20 x 20 cm) (or similar size) baking dish lined with parchment paper.

5. Bake for 20 minutes, or until a toothpick comes out clean in the center.

Tip The date paste can also be made in the microwave if you're short on time. Just combine the dates with ½ tablespoon (7 ml) of water in a microwave-safe bowl and heat for 30 seconds. Remove the bowl from the microwave, then add the remaining water and mash into a paste.

seven

Drinks
in a Dash

This chapter includes some of my favorite beverages to take you through your day,
starting with your morning coffee, all the way through to happy hour with friends. Start your
day with a creamy Coconut Milk Iced Vanilla Latte (page 153) or Vitalizing Morning Lemonade
(page 154), and end it with Honey Lime Margaritas (page 157) or a Hot Chocolate (page 161).

COCONUT MILK ICED *Vanilla* LATTE

When the weather starts getting warmer, I have only one thing on my mind: iced coffee! The coconut milk adds a thick creaminess to this drink that gets me up and moving at the start of a busy day!

YIELD: 1 drink

2-2-23

INGREDIENTS

8 oz (240 ml) coffee, chilled

6–7 ice cubes

Dash of vanilla extract

3 drops stevia, optional

¼ cup (60 ml) full-fat canned coconut milk

DIRECTIONS

1. Pour the coffee over the ice and add vanilla and stevia (optional).

2. Mix in the coconut milk.

Tip For an even thicker drink, try blending all of the ingredients together in a high-speed blender.

Vitalizing Morning Lemonade

Lemon is naturally refreshing, but combining it with the other stellar ingredients in this recipe is what makes this beverage so delicious. Drink it in the morning to wake up your system, or throughout the day for a revitalizing blend with an extra kick.

YIELD: 1 DRINK

INGREDIENTS

1 cup (240 ml) water
1 tbsp (15 ml) lemon juice
1 tbsp (15 ml) apple cider vinegar
½ tbsp (7 g) honey
Sprinkle of cayenne pepper

DIRECTIONS

1. Combine all the ingredients in a large glass over ice.

Tip Substitute 3–4 drops of liquid stevia for the honey for a lower-sugar version.

Honey Lime Margaritas

If I could have only one drink for the rest of my life, it would probably be these margaritas. They're nice and light, unlike the pre-mixed varieties you find at the store, and they're a huge hit for Cinco de Mayo (or let's be honest, pretty much any happy hour)! A little lemon, a little lime and a bit of honey combine to bring you this cool, refreshing cocktail.

YIELD: 5 DRINKS

INGREDIENTS

12 oz (360 ml) lime juice

4 oz (120 ml) lemon juice

½ cup (168 g) honey

1 cup (240 ml) water

10 oz (300 ml) tequila

5 oz (150 ml) Cointreau

Ice, to serve

DIRECTIONS

1. Combine the lime juice, lemon juice, honey and water in a high-speed blender for 30 seconds.

2. Mix in the tequila and Cointreau.

3. Serve over ice.

Tip You don't need to be 21 or older to enjoy this beverage. Omit the alcohol for a fun "mocktail" version!

Sleepy Time GOLDEN MILK

This yummy spiced milk can be served hot or cold depending on your preference, which makes it great for sipping year-round! Drink it warmed on a cold winter evening or cooled for a summertime treat.

YIELD: 1 DRINK

INGREDIENTS

1 cup (240 ml) unsweetened almond milk

½ tbsp (8 ml) coconut oil

1 tsp maple syrup

Dash of vanilla extract

½ tsp ground turmeric

½ tsp ground cinnamon

DIRECTIONS

1. Combine all of the ingredients in a small saucepan over medium heat and whisk continuously until smooth.

2. Reduce the heat to low and simmer for at least 5 minutes before serving, stirring occasionally. Allow to cool if desired.

Hot Chocolate

There's nothing better than curling up by the fireplace with a warm cup of hot cocoa in the cold winter months. This rich, creamy hot chocolate takes under 2 minutes to prepare and will warm you up in no time!

Yield: 1 drink

. . . .

Ingredients

1 cup (240 ml) unsweetened almond milk

3 tbsp (15 g) cocoa powder

1 tbsp (21 g) honey

Dash of vanilla extract

Dash of sea salt

Directions

1. Combine all the ingredients in a small saucepan over medium heat and whisk continuously until the cocoa has dissolved and all the ingredients are well-combined, about 3–4 minutes.

eight

EASY
EXTRAS

A little bit of this and a little bit of that, the recipes in this section include condiments and "extras" that add flavor and fun to main meals and snacks. From my All Purpose Pizza Crust (page 174) to the Homemade Basil Pesto (page 166), these add-ons can enhance a variety of dishes from this book and beyond.

Cheesy CASHEW CREAM

It's okay if you want to bathe in this cashew cream, really. It's soft, creamy and delicious with a "cheesy" essence that will have you addicted in no time. Use it as a sauce in spiralized veggie noodle dishes or as a dip for raw veggies. The possibilities are endless!

YIELD: ABOUT 3 CUPS (362 G)

3-19-23 good

INGREDIENTS

2 cups (225 g) raw cashews

3 ¼ cups (300 ml) water, divided

¼ cup (20 g) Dijon mustard

¼ cup (15 g) nutritional yeast

2 tbsp (30 ml) apple cider vinegar

1 tsp garlic, minced

½ tsp sea salt

Pepper to taste

DIRECTIONS

1. Soak the cashews in 2 cups (480 ml) of water for at least 2 hours (overnight is best if you have the time).

2. Drain the cashews, then add them to a food processor along with the remaining water, Dijon mustard, nutritional yeast, vinegar, garlic, salt and pepper and blend on high until very smooth, about 2–3 minutes.

Tip You can make this sauce without soaking the cashews at all if you're in a pinch. It won't be quite as creamy, but it will be just as delicious!

Homemade Basil Pesto

I started growing my own basil plant a couple of summers ago, and that's how my true love
of this homemade pesto came to be. I love being able to go outside and pick herbs right off of the stem to incorporate
into dinner that night. Not to mention, the smell of fresh basil is totally intoxicating to me! (If I could make a
perfume out of it, I totally would.) This pesto is so versatile and can be used in so many different recipes to give things
a kick of freshness. Try it on the Spaghetti Squash Vegetable Pizza Bake on page 42
or in the Pesto Chicken and Summer Veggie Packets on page 104.

YIELD: ½ CUP (76 G)

. . . .

INGREDIENTS

¼ cup (38 g) pine nuts

4 cups (70 g) fresh basil, lightly packed

1 tsp garlic, minced

¼ cup (60 ml) olive oil

Salt and pepper to taste

DIRECTIONS

1. Combine all the ingredients in a food processor and blend on high until creamy, about 1 minute.

Tip Depending on the size of your food processor, you may need to stop the blending periodically to scrape down the sides of the bowl, and then start again.

My Go-To Taco Seasoning

I call this "taco" seasoning, but it can really be used in any Mexican dish. I most often use it for seasoning whatever protein I choose for taco night, but the just-spicy-enough flavor is great on veggies, in soups, etc. Try it in the Mexican Fiesta Skillet on page 45.

YIELD: HEAPING ¼ CUP (60 G)

INGREDIENTS

2 tbsp (18 g) chili powder

1 tbsp (12 g) cumin

2 tsp (12 g) sea salt

2 tsp (4 g) black pepper

1 tsp paprika

½ tsp dried oregano

½ tsp garlic powder

½ tsp onion powder

½ tsp red pepper flakes

DIRECTIONS

1. Combine all of the spices.

2. Store in an airtight container.

Spicy "Peanut" Sauce

I love making my own sauces because you never know what kind of sneaky ingredients can be found in those from stores or restaurants. I love the Thai flavor this sauce brings to recipes, but I also love adding it to any protein or veggie for a little extra kick!

YIELD: 1 ¼ CUPS (300 G)

INGREDIENTS

½ cup (128 g) almond butter

¼ cup (60 ml) coconut aminos

¼ cup (60 ml) water

1–2 tsp (5–10 g) Sriracha

1 tsp coconut sugar

½ tsp garlic, minced

¼ tsp fresh ginger, grated

¼ tsp sea salt

DIRECTIONS

1. Whisk all the ingredients together in a small bowl until smooth.

Tip If you aren't a fan of spicy foods, omit the Sriracha altogether for a mild flavor. And if you like more heat, increase it slowly until you reach your desired level of spiciness.

Blackberry Chia Jam

My mom has always loved having jam on her toast in the morning, but she has always struggled to find a store-bought version with a "clean" ingredient list. Try this homemade version as a sweet spread on the Honey Almond Flax Loaf (page 24) or the Pumpkin Spice Waffles (page 28).

YIELD: 1 CUP (230 G)

INGREDIENTS

2 ½ cups (277 g) fresh blackberries

2 tbsp (30 ml) water

2 tbsp (24 g) coconut sugar

1 tsp lemon juice

1 tbsp (12 g) chia seeds

DIRECTIONS

1. Combine all of the ingredients except for the chia seeds in a saucepan over medium heat.

2. Using a fork, mash the blackberries down a bit while stirring frequently.

3. Remove from the heat and allow to cool for 5 minutes.

4. Stir in the chia seeds and place the mixture in the refrigerator. Allow to set until gelled, at least one hour.

Tip You can sub any berry you'd like in this recipe! Try strawberries, raspberries or blueberries when you want to switch things up.

All Purpose Pizza Crust

You'll be whipping up homemade pizzas every weekend once you try this yummy crust! The almond flour base makes it crispy, flakey and the perfect vessel for any and all topping combinations you can dream up.

YIELD: 1 CRUST

INGREDIENTS

2 cups (224 g) almond meal

2 large eggs

2 tbsp (30 ml) olive oil

1 tsp sea salt

½ cup (40 g) nutritional yeast

DIRECTIONS

Preheat oven to 350°F (176°C).

1. Combine all of the ingredients in a large bowl and mix to form a dough.

2. Form a ball with the dough and place it between two large sheets of parchment paper. Using a rolling pin, roll the dough out into a ⅙-inch (4-mm) thick crust.

3. Remove the top piece of parchment paper and place the bottom piece with the crust on top onto a baking sheet.

4. Bake for 10 minutes.

5. Top with the desired ingredients and return to the oven as directed.

Tip Remember, pizzas come in all shapes and sizes. Don't worry if your crust isn't a perfect circle or square! However, if you are aiming for perfection, you can always cut off the edges with a knife for that picture-perfect presentation!

Honey Dijon Vinaigrette

Skip the store-bought dressing and whip up a batch of your own that easily pairs with any flavor. This sweet and tangy blend takes just seconds to make and adds a light and refreshing note to any salad.

YIELD: 1 CUP (240 ML)

INGREDIENTS

¼ cup + 2 tbsp (90 ml) olive oil

1 tbsp (15 ml) white vinegar

1 tbsp (15 ml) water

½ tsp garlic, minced

2 tsp (14 g) honey

2 tsp (10 g) Dijon mustard

¼ tsp sea salt

¼ tsp pepper

DIRECTIONS

1. Combine all the ingredients in a small bowl and whisk to combine.

2. Store in the refrigerator.

Tip The oil will separate from the other ingredients after storing. But not to worry, this is perfectly normal! Just give it a shake before your next use.

Two-Ingredient HONEY MUSTARD SAUCE

Honey mustard was always my favorite condiment as a kid, and now I can love it again as an adult!
The sweet, zingy taste is still one of my favorites, and with just two ingredients, this version is
a no-brainer to have on hand in the fridge at all times.

YIELD: ¾ CUP (184 G)

easy + good 3/28/23

INGREDIENTS
½ cup (60 g) Dijon mustard

¼ cup (60 ml) honey

DIRECTIONS
1. Mix the ingredients together until well combined.

> **Tip** Keep this sauce refrigerated in an air-tight container to maximize its storage life.

ACKNOWLEDGMENTS

A heartfelt thank you to my mom and dad, my number one taste-testers who have always supported me in any venture I take on. Especially to my "Sue" chef, who has cleaned too many dishes to count during this entire cookbook-writing process (which deserves an entire award in itself). You guys are truly the best.

To the rest of my family and friends who have tried my recipes, helped me edit this book and have kept me sane during the entire journey, thank you all for being you.

To Allie and Adam, without whom this book wouldn't be anywhere near as beautiful as it is. Thank you for your passion, expertise and kindness throughout this entire project. It no doubt shines through on every page.

To Simi and Tim, thank you for lending me your beautiful kitchen (shown throughout the chapters in this book) to laugh and cook in.

To the team at Page Street, for presenting me with this incredible opportunity. Thank you for making my visions for this book a reality.

And most importantly, thank you to the readers of my blog. I would have never had this opportunity without all of your endless support over the years, and I hope this book can serve as a small gift of my appreciation to each and every one of you. Words will never describe how grateful I feel for you all!

ABOUT THE AUTHOR

TAYLOR RIGGS is a Registered Dietitian and the author of the healthy living blog, *Simply Taylor*, through which she shares her passion for balanced, healthy living one recipe at a time.

Living with type 1 diabetes since the age of ten, nutrition has always played a large role in her life and, over time, has helped her learn that food can truly be our best medicine.

Taylor was born and raised in Columbus, Ohio, where she currently lives and works as a dietitian nutritionist.

INDEX